Simplifying Life as a Senior Citizen

Also by Joan Cleveland

Everything You Need to Know About Retirement Housing

SIMPLIFYING LIFE AS A SENIOR CITIZEN

HUNDREDS OF TIPS TO MAKE EVERYDAY LIVING EASIER

Joan Cleveland

Illustrations by Curtiss Calleo

St. Martin's Griffin ❧ *New York*

Library of Congress Cataloging-in-Publication Data

Cleveland, Joan.
    Simplifying life as a senior citizen : hundreds of tips to make everyday living easier / by Joan Cleveland : with illustrations by Curtiss Calleo.
        p.   cm.
    Includes bibliographical references.
    ISBN 0-312-18758-0
    1. Aged—United States—Life skills guides.   I. Title.
HQ1064.U5C515   1998   98-12949
646.7'00846—dc21   CIP

First St. Martin's Griffin Edition: July 1998

10 9 8 7 6 5 4 3 2 1

To Alice, my companion and guide in the challenge of making things easier, and to the memory of her grandmother, Marian van Buren Cleveland, with whom I learned that with ingenuity, persistence, and good humor you can do almost anything.

Contents

Acknowledgments

This book might never have happened without the enthusiasm, help, and encouragement of many people. I thank, especially, Marion Clifford, surely one of the world's most persistent and effective problem solvers; Jane Compton and G. Rockwood Clark, who helped immeasurably with the garden chapter; Carolyn Shaw Bell and her Hearing Ear dog, Robin, who taught me much about how to cope with deafness; Sheila O'Brian and her staff at NEADs, who introduced me to the myriad ways four-legged helpers can help; Frederick Sherman, M.D., Associate Director of Geriatrics at Mount Sinai Hospital in New York, who generously shared his experience and wisdom; Jennie Thompson of *The Today Show,* who provided reassurance that this subject is really of vital interest to millions of people; Jeanne Blackman, Policy Advisor to the Attorney General of Illinois for

Senior Issues, who taught me much about fraud; and Amy Kephart and Heath Smith, who lived through the writing of this book with unfailing support and sympathy.

Without my wise and patient literary agent, Heidi von Schreiner of Pen and Pixel, this book would never have been written. Heather Jackson, my editor at St. Martin's Press, gently made it a much better book.

Finally, I must acknowledge my debt to three special people who have shaped my thinking and attitudes about finding ways to do things and making things work: Cecilie Birner and Fosdick, who live with more problems than I can contemplate and who nonetheless lead happy, productive, full, and altogether remarkable lives. They give new meaning to the word *cope* and personify the motto that a problem is something with a solution. And my daughter, Alice, to whom this book is dedicated, who has made a profession of understanding how things work and making them work better.

Introduction

As we get older, some systems work better and some not as well. We are all painfully aware of the ones that don't work—joints that ache, hands that shake, eyes that don't see and ears that don't hear as well as they used to. But sadly, we don't focus nearly as clearly on the systems that work better—knowledge, experience, wisdom. We know more and have more sense than we used to.

This book proceeds from my belief that a problem is something with a solution—that's how you tell it from a catastrophe. My goal is to help you get through the day and do all the things you need or want to do. It's not to help you act as if you are thirty years younger than you are or to deny problems that we all have that we didn't used to have. We may be older, but we're smarter too.

The problems we may be encountering as we age are not numerous—we are likely to be experiencing some deterioration in moving and motor coordination, in seeing, hearing, and smelling, and in memory. That's not a very long list. Similarly, what we need, or want to be able to do, isn't a very long list either. We need to get up in the morning, bathe and dress in clothes that are in wearable condition, get meals on the table, and get around. Those are the only things we *need* to do. Gardening, staying in touch with friends and dear ones, going out to meals, movies, church, reading and watching TV are among the things we want to do. This book will take you through all of these activities with lots of suggestions about how to do the things you need to and the things you want to do within the new limits of your abilities.

But before that, I urge you to look carefully at those limits. Whenever you think "I can't," ask yourself who says you can't. Very often we're told we can't do something by some well-meaning caregiver who happens to be wrong. Only you know what you really can do if you want to and try hard enough. You may decide that you can't, or that you don't want to. That's fine. But don't take someone else's word for it, even if the someone else is a medical professional or a caretaker. Medical profession-als—doctors and nurses—may be good at treating diseases, but they may be no better than the rest of us at living with them. Caregivers are concerned for you, but one of the ways that concern sometimes manifests itself is by taking control of your life. (It's a good thing your mother didn't take that position when you were learning to walk. You never would have fallen, but you also never would have learned to walk.) Nobody but you should be in control of your life. What you can do is often a function of what you think you can do.

Maybe the real truth is not that you can't, but just that you can't the old way. If, for example, you have become hard of hearing, the old way of having a conversation won't work for you anymore. But you can learn to lip-read and have conversations a new way. You just have to decide whether having conversations is worth the trouble of learning to lip-read. That's your choice, and you really must make it. Remember that by making the choice, you are staying in charge of your life and deciding what you are going to do with your time and energy. Making choices for yourself keeps you from being a victim. Of course, if your hearing is gone, that is a fact of life that you have to acknowledge. But you are still in charge of deciding what to do about it—how much you let it affect your life.

Pay attention to all the preconceived notions people have about "old people" and pay particular attention to how many of them you have bought into. It is not true that old people can't learn—you *can* teach old dogs new tricks, to say nothing of old people. Of course, it takes time and energy to learn new things. It always has. Students think they are the most overworked people on earth. But you have as much time as you need, and if you haven't as much energy as you once did, learn with whatever energy you have, rest awhile, then learn some more. The thrill of knowing something—including knowing how to do something—today that you didn't know yesterday is one of life's greatest pleasures, and you never, *never* get too old to experience it.

The fact that you're reading this book suggests that, in your heart of hearts, you know you can do the things you want to do. You are just discouraged by the amount of ingenuity and learning it requires. Don't be. Instead of thinking about it as daunting, think about it as an adventure. Better yet, think about it as a bit of self-indulgence. Say to yourself, "Who says I can't? I want to!"

I learned this lesson a few years ago when I broke my right wrist two days before Thanksgiving. My right hand—the only one that knows how to do anything—was to be totally immobilized and unusable for six weeks, through the New Year. I like to cook and feed people at Thanksgiving and Christmas, and I had neither bought nor wrapped any Christmas presents. So I pouted for an hour and whined about how unfair it was. Then I decided to figure out how to deal with it.

As it happened, I had invited a friend for dinner the night of my accident. Of course, we could have changed our plans and gone out for dinner. But I really couldn't imagine having to go out for all my meals for six weeks, as it would have guaranteed an absolutely unacceptable increase in my waistline and concomitant decrease in my bank account. (The rule is that you can't be too thin or too rich, not the reverse.) So I figured out a meal I could cook with one hand, and I was off and running. I learned during that period that it is accurate to describe people with physical problems as challenged—that's exactly what it is, a challenge. At first, it seemed as if a hundred times a day I thought, "Okay. There's something the matter with your hand, not with your brain. If you're so smart, figure out how to do it without the hand." In the end, the only thing I couldn't do with one hand was put my watch on, and I could have gotten another watchband that would have allowed me to do that too.

But I noticed the subtle sabotage I got from my nearest and dearest. My plans called for me to drive the day after the accident, with a carful of dogs and a cat, to my house in the country. It's about a five-hour trip. Everyone clucked and said, "Oh, you can't possibly." I thought, Generations of young men have driven with one hand. When I do it, at least I will be paying attention to where I am going, which is more than you can say for most of them. So the next day, I piled the critters and the makings of a Thanksgiving feast into the car, and off I went. I'm not going to lie and tell you it was no trouble. It was a nuisance. Every time I wanted to change the radio station or turn the heat up or down I had to pull off the road. I couldn't drink a cup of coffee while driving. The trip probably took an extra hour with all this stopping. But I got there. And I felt triumphant. I had met the challenge. You can too.

One of the things challenges do for you is make you focus on what you really want, because it's not worth the trouble to meet the challenge in order to do something that doesn't matter. That's where the wiser part of aging comes in. We have all probably spent thousands of hours and endless amounts of energy doing things which, in retrospect, seem foolish. If you've forgotten, just watch a teenager get ready for a dance! The fact that something is more difficult to do makes you stop a minute to consider whether it's really worth doing. If it isn't, forget it. But if it is, spend the extra energy figuring out how. Taking a moment to answer the question, "Does it really matter?" helps put things in perspective and helps eliminate a lot of time and energy spent on things that return neither pleasure nor utility.

As you go through this book, pay attention to how you have lived lo these many years. If you haven't cooked dinner in decades, skip the kitchen chapter, unless you're looking for a new hobby. If you have always had a black thumb, it may not be worth learning to garden when you can't bend or lift. (There are hints in the gardening section, though, that will allow you to have a breathtaking garden with barely any work. Won't they be surprised!)

But before you decide you can't do something you *want* to do, read the relevant chapter. It may not be necessary to give up doing things that you enjoy because something has happened to your physical equipment. Simplifying your life doesn't mean diminishing it. Quite the reverse: It means getting rid of unimportant things and focusing on what matters—the things that give you pleasure or satisfaction.

I
Practical Matters

1

A KINDER, GENTLER PLACE

HINTS ON HOW TO BE MORE COMFORTABLE AND SAFER IN YOUR HOME

Home is the place where we feel cozy and safe, so it is distressing to consider that it is also the place where you are most likely to hurt yourself. More accidents occur at home than anywhere else. However, there are many ways to make your home safe. I deal with kitchens and bathrooms—the most dangerous places of all—in separate chapters. But your house and grounds are probably also full of inconveniences and even dangers, many of which you can fix with a little attention and a small amount of money. Let's look at ways to make your home safer and then consider ways to make it more convenient.

Although there are myriad ways you can fall victim to them, there are really only four ways to get hurt in your house—falls, fire, fumes, and felonies!

FALLS

Although they may be amusing in slapstick comedies, falls are not funny at all. They put more people in nursing homes than any other sort of accident or illness. There are many common reasons for falls at home, but perhaps the most frequent is that you can't see where you're going. Our Depression Era upbringing notwithstanding, it is *not* a waste of money to leave lights on.

Photosensors, which go on when it's dark, should turn lights on automatically in every
- room
- hallway
- staircase

Motion sensors, which go on when something moves, should be installed in

❑ the path from your bed to the bathroom

❑ the path to the attic and cellar

A remote-control device should let you turn on the light in your front hall or living room from fifty feet away—keep the transmitter on your key chain!

Keep a flashlight in every room in the house, in case of a power failure.

❑ If your living room is illuminated only by lamps that aren't activated by wall switches, you can install a wall switch next to the entrance to the living room. You plug the lamp into a special device (really a receiver unit) that you plug into a wall outlet. Then you fasten the wall switch to the wall, with either screws or tape, both of which are provided. You can then turn on the lamps either with the wall switch or with a handheld transmitter that you can keep on your key chain. You don't need an electrician to do this, and the unit costs about $35.

❑ Get a lamp that turns on when you clap your hands!

❑ A lamp that turns on whenever you touch it might be nice to have next to your bed.

❑ Replace ordinary switches with rocker switches, which are easier for stiff fingers to operate.

❑ Get a gadget that lets you turn on the light from a sitting position (great for wheelchair users and a help if getting up out of a chair is a strain).

Lights No Home Should Be Without

❑ an outdoor light that comes on when it gets dark

❑ motion-sensor outdoor lights that come on when something moves

❑ a motion-sensor light in the entryway that comes on when something moves

❑ living room lights you can turn on with a transmitter on your key chain

- ❑ motion-sensor lights that illuminate the way from bedroom to bathroom
- ❑ lights on timers that go on at dusk in main rooms, hallways, and stairs
- ❑ motion-sensor lights in the attic and the cellar
- ❑ lights that work off batteries in the event of a power outage near your bed, your favorite chair, and the front door

Avoiding Falls

Other major reasons for falls at home are the surfaces you walk on and the things you trip over.

Chief culprits are area rugs.

- ❑ Buy superstrong rug pads with dry adhesive to keep your rugs flat.
- ❑ Get two-sided tape at any hardware store and tape down the rugs.
- ❑ If you have a rug that really can't be secured, *get rid of it!* Or hang it on the wall.

Bare floors can be dangerous too.

❏ Don't wax wood floors.

❏ Marble and tile floors are slippery when wet—keep a mop nearby.

❏ Mix a little sand in the varnish you put on your floor to increase traction.

❏ Roughen the soles of new shoes with sandpaper before you wear them.

Be careful not to trip.

❏ If you have thresholds just high enough to trip over, remove them and replace them with a piece of wood that is flush with the floor, or paint them in a contrasting color so you can see them.

❏ Keep clutter off the floor by having a few wicker baskets around the house to put shoes and newspapers in.

❏ Keep furniture out of traffic paths, especially paths to the phone and door.

Make your furniture work for you.

❏ Furniture next to your bed or chair should be sturdy enough to lean on while you are standing up or sitting down.

❏ If getting up is hard, there are chairs that catapult you to a standing position (there are also cushions that do this, to take with you when you're traveling).

❏ If your chair is too low for comfort, get leg extenders.

If you spend a lot of time sitting, think about getting an ergonomic chair, especially if you have back trouble.

❏ Seat height should be adjustable.

❏ The depth of the seat should be about two-thirds the length of your thighs and buttocks.

❏ The seat cushion should be of dense and resilient foam rubber, and the front edge should be rounded.

❏ The back must be at least fourteen inches high—twenty-one inches is better—and it should be easily adjustable.

❏ The armrests should be no more than eight or nine inches high.

One of the most important devices in your home is your telephone, which links you to the rest of the world.

❑ Do you have extension phones where you need them—in the kitchen, in the bathroom, near your favorite chair, near your bed?

❑ Can you reach the phone from the floor? If you fall and can't stand up, you may still be able to crawl.

❑ Do you have a panic button that you wear as a pendant around your neck? To find companies that sell and service these, look under "Medical Alarms, Systems & Monitoring" in the Yellow Pages.

Falls commonly happen when you are reaching for things in awkward places or walking with your arms full.

❑ Remove items from high shelves with grabbers.

❑ If you must climb, use a ladder, *not a chair*.

❑ Always keep a hand free for steadying yourself.

❑ Carry things around on wheeled carts or in a suitcase with wheels.

Finally, the most serious cause of falls—stairs.

❑ You should really not climb stairs, even if it means moving.

❑ If you must use stairs daily, think about getting a stair lift. Stair lifts range in price from $2,000 to $20,000, and they work best on straight stairs.

❑ Be sure to have sturdy banisters, ideally on both sides.

❑ Cover stairs with securely installed carpeting or another nonskid surface.

❑ Would a little refrigerator and a coffeepot upstairs cut down the number of trips you make up and down the stairs each day?

❑ Keep a basket at the top and bottom of the stairs so you have a place to put things that have to be taken up- and downstairs. This way you won't leave them on the floor to trip over. A basket with a handle that you can put over your arm is best.

Falls outside happen for all the reasons falls indoors happen—and a few more. So take a look at the outside of your house.

❏ *Any* route you take home after dark—from the street to your front door or from the garage to the inside of the house—should have lights that go on automatically, in response either to darkness or to motion.

❏ Don't forget the path from the kitchen door to the garbage can.

❏ Keep a flashlight near each door, in case of a power failure.

❏ Outdoor activities, like barbecuing, should be well lit.

❏ A few outside lights, with switches inside the house, can help you identify strange noises or neighboring dogs from the safety of your living room or kitchen.

❏ If visiting dogs or other animals are a chronic problem for you, get a motion-sensor device that turns on the sprinkler and sprays them with cold water—which should discourage return visits!

❏ If you have a garage, use it! You are much less likely to fall on a dry garage floor than on an icy or wet driveway.

Outside surfaces can be tricky, as they are often paths made of gravel or flagstone—which by their very nature are apt to be bumpy. Examine your property, noting *every place* that can cause you to stumble. Then sit down, perhaps with your contractor, and figure out how to smooth each of them.

❑ Flagstones may have to be set in cement to hold them firm and level.

❑ Should gravel paths be replaced with paved ones?

❑ Would small rocks, painted white, along paths make them easier to see?

If you live in a part of the country where it snows, review the paths to and from your home and car with that in mind.

❑ Remove snow with a snow scoop that you push instead of lift.

❑ Or use a snowblower if you're nervous about slipping.

❑ Cat litter sprinkled on the path will give you traction and not ruin your planting, like salt, or attract rodents, like birdseed. Keep a bag near each door and one in the car.

No matter how well you maintain your grounds, unless you are willing to stay home all winter, you will have to rely on other people's snow-clearing prowess.

❑ Don't leave home without cleats that you can strap over your shoes.

❑ Always wear appropriate footgear—hiking boots or sneakers—and carry your chic shoes to change into if you must.

A snow scoop that you push, not lift.

FIRE

There are few things in the world more terrifying than fire, but it is relatively easy to safeguard against the most common causes of home fires.

- ❑ Keep your wiring in good repair and don't overload circuits or outlets.
- ❑ Don't use lamps or appliances with frayed cords.
- ❑ Have smoke alarms in your kitchen and bedrooms. Replace the batteries twice a year, when you turn your clocks ahead or back.
- ❑ Have a fire extinguisher in the kitchen, in the garage, and next to the fireplace.
- ❑ Never leave home while a heat-producing appliance, like an oven or a clothes dryer, is running—don't trust it to turn itself off!
- ❑ Storing pots on the top of the stove makes it hard to see if the burner is still on.
- ❑ Don't leave lights on in closets and keep piles of clothes and linens away from the lightbulb.

If you tend to be absentminded about remembering that appliances are on, here are a few tips:

❑ Get an electric coffeepot with a thermos instead of a carafe. Then, when you take that first cup, turn off the coffeepot. The thermos keeps the coffee hot all day, and it tastes better than if it is allowed to sit on a heating surface.

❑ Keep a timer on a cord next to the dryer. Whenever you put it on, set the timer and put it around your neck to remind you.

At Christmas, blazing pudding is fine, but blazing trees are another matter.

❑ Never put candles on or near the tree.

❑ You can get a gadget that has a funnel at a convenient height attached to tubing that goes into the water receptacle of your Christmas tree. This allows you to replace water as it evaporates, without gymnastics.

❑ A fire alarm, made to look like a Christmas tree ball, will sound if the temperature rises above 113°F.

❑ Don't leave the lights on the tree burning when you leave the room.

FUMES

As we get older, the quality and purity of the air in our homes becomes more important because

❑ Upper respiratory problems become more serious.

❑ We tend to spend more time at home.

❑ Our sense of smell becomes less acute.

You can get devices that test for dangerous substances in the air:

❑ a carbon monoxide detector—you need this if you have a furnace

❑ a combustible gas detector—you need this unless you live in an all-electric world

❑ a radon detector—you need this if you live in an area where radon is present

If you find something in your air that doesn't belong there, or if you are allergic and need very clean air, you might want to get an air filter. The good ones are not inexpensive, nor are the filters, although a filter lasts for months or years.

Depending on the size of your home, you can get an air cleaner for less than $500 (or $1,000 if you have a large home), which may be a very good investment. Some multipurpose filtering devices cool and humidify the air as well. Especially if you are spending more time at home than you used to, it might be worth a little trouble and money to make the air you breathe cleaner and more comfortable.

FELONIES

It is regrettable but true that older people are targeted by criminals more often than younger ones. Even if you live in a gated community with guards, you would do well to look around your home to make sure it is as safe as it can be.

Light is the enemy of crime. People who are up to no good rarely choose to do their mischief under a spotlight.

❑ Install motion-sensor lights around your property. (They will be switched on frequently by rabbits running across the lawn,

so don't panic just because the light comes
on!)

❑ Place a few lights around the perimeter of
your property.

Light makes shadows, which are good hiding
places.

❑ Avoid tall shrubbery near the door.

❑ Install mirrors to help you see blind spots.

The house itself should be made secure.

❑ Doors and windows should be securely
locked, even when you are at home.

❑ Doors should have dead bolts and hinges that
can't be removed from the outside.

❑ Install a peephole so you can see who is on
the other side of the door.

❑ A sturdy door is heavy, so you may want to
get a door-opening device that opens your
door at the touch of a button.

Think about an alarm system. There are basi-
cally two kinds. One just makes noise when it is
violated, but unless you live in a very densely

populated place, that probably won't be adequate for your needs. The other sends an alarm, sometimes a silent one, to the service that you have engaged to monitor your system. They will notify the police or fire department, as appropriate. The cost of monitoring varies widely (some companies install the equipment at no charge if you sign a monitoring contract with them) because it essentially rests on the cost of labor in the area where you live. If you wear a pendant for emergencies, which we discussed earlier in this chapter, you may feel you don't need a burglar alarm system as well. Certainly, a crime in progress is up there with a fall as a genuine emergency!

- ❑ Ask your local police department to do a security check of your home.
- ❑ Start a neighborhood watch if you don't have one.

MAKE YOUR HOME A HAPPIER PLACE TO LIVE

This is your home, and it should be what you want it to be. (It's not necessary to worry anymore that your mother-in-law approve your color scheme.)

❑ Have pretty cotton slipcovers made for your furniture, so you don't have to worry about spills. If the slipcover gets soiled, wash it in cold water and put it back on the furniture damp. It will dry with nary a wrinkle.

❑ Carpeting is easier to clean than wood floors.

❑ You may find that a cordless vacuum cleaner is easier to use on your carpets as it has no cord to trip over.

❑ Instead of making your bed, replace the top sheet, blanket, and bedspread with a duvet—then shake it to make it.

❑ Make your bed as soon as you get out of it. For some reason, the longer you wait to make a bed the harder it is to do it—by late afternoon it's nearly impossible!

❏ Insulated draperies or shades make your home cozier.

❏ Good storm windows keep heat in and dust out.

❏ Keep bowls of potpourri around the house and run your hand through them from time to time to release the scent into the air.

❏ Pay attention to the amount of moisture in the air. Cozy homes tend to have dry air in winter, and you might want to get a humidifier or put pans of water on top of your radiators.

If you have trouble getting a fire going, try these tricks:

❏ Wrap a few candle ends in the newspaper you put under the kindling.

❏ After you have lit the balled-up newspaper under the twigs, place a flat sheet of newspaper over the whole thing and light that. It will draw air up through the kindling and make it burn better (Don't do this if you live in a very dry climate! Pieces of burning paper might go up the chimney and fall on dry grass.)

If you want to be surrounded by fragrant flowers all winter:

- ❑ Buy hyacinth, paper-white, and amaryllis bulbs.
- ❑ Store the bulbs in the refrigerator.
- ❑ Every few weeks, take out a few bulbs and plant them in pebbles and water.
- ❑ Keep the water level at the top of the pebbles.

The warmth of the room will fool them into thinking it's spring, and you will have fresh flowers all winter.

Hint: You can keep cut flowers fresh for incredibly long periods of time if you put them in a solution of half water and half lemon soda, like Sprite, Slice, or 7-Up.

No matter how pleasant and cozy your home is, it will not make you happy if you are lonely. There are many ways to deal with living alone if you don't like it.

Find a housemate to share your home and the expenses of running it. The housemate will expect his or her own bedroom and will expect to share the public areas, like the living room and kitchen. You can work out any arrangement you like concerning what meals you have together, how you deal with each other's guests, and how much responsibility you each take for the other. Housemates seem to work out best when they are acquaintances who like each other and have interests and tastes in common but who are not very close friends. You should do some things together and some separately, and neither of you should be made to feel that if you go out with friends or visit your grandchildren, you are somehow abandoning the other one. Housemates usually find each other by word of mouth, or through churches or senior centers, although in big cities there are sometimes real estate agents who specialize in finding roommates. You can also send an SASE to National Shared Housing Resource Center, 321 East 25 Street, Baltimore, MD 21218.

If you don't think you want quite so much of a

relationship, but you'd like somebody under your roof and you'd like a little income, maybe you want to rent a room or two. Boarders are likely to be less involved in your life than a housemate.

If you require services, you might be able to find somebody who, in exchange for room and board, will do chores for you, walk the dog, get dinner every night, or run errands.

Questions to Ask
a Potential Housemate

- ❑ What kinds of food, drink, music, do you like?
- ❑ What are your favorite TV programs?
- ❑ What are your hobbies and interests?
- ❑ Do you smoke and/or drink?
- ❑ Do you tidy up immediately, hourly, daily, rarely, never?

The answers to these questions should be similar enough to the answers you would give so that you will be comfortable together. If you are relaxed about cleaning, for example, you may have trouble living with somebody who does the dishes between courses!

Cleaning Up Your Act

If you are spending more time at home now, you may find that keeping your home clean and neat is more important than it used to be. It may also be harder. Here are some ways to tackle cleaning jobs in ways that won't leave you exhausted.

Neat is not the same as clean, but it's easier to achieve!

❑ Get a few decorative baskets to hold magazines, newspapers, scarves, and all the other things that litter your landscape.

❑ Take a careful look at the things you have around your home. Do you get pleasure, or use, from all of them? Anything that doesn't qualify as either pleasurable or useful doesn't deserve house room. Put it away or give it away.

Don't try to clean the whole house at once. If you neaten it every morning and clean one room each day, the job won't be overwhelming.

The right equipment makes cleaning easier.

❑ Get a feather duster or lamb's wool duster with a long handle.

❑ Sponge mops don't have to be wrung out by hand—they come with a lever that lets you squeeze them dry. (Be sure to buy several refill sponges when you buy the mop. Finding refills when you need them is often a nuisance.)

❑ Get a dustpan with a long handle so you can pick up sweepings without bending.

❑ A vacuum cleaner with a wand attachment will make it easier to dust moldings and the tops of pictures and furniture.

❑ An effortless way to dust is to put an old cotton glove or sock, sprayed with a little furniture polish, on each hand. Then just rub your hands over the furniture.

Keep all your cleaning supplies and equipment in a basket and move it around with you on a wheeled cart or table. Don't try to carry it—it will be heavy.

Let the wonders of science help you in the kitchen:

- ❑ For food burned onto pots, put some water in the pot and add about a half cup of vinegar and two tablespoons of baking soda. Bring to a boil and simmer for half an hour. The burned-on food will come right off.
- ❑ For food burned onto the oven or broiler, sprinkle with dishwashing detergent, cover with damp paper towels and leave for a few hours.
- ❑ If you drop an egg on the floor, sprinkle it heavily with salt and wait a few minutes. Then sweep it up.
- ❑ If your drain gets clogged, pour in a cup each of baking soda and vinegar followed by a kettleful of boiling water.
- ❑ If you have stacked glasses and they get stuck, fill the top one with ice cubes or very cold water and set the bottom one in very hot water. After a minute or two they should come apart easily.

Protect your skin.

❏ Wear rubber gloves when you use cleaning products.

❏ Get a dishwashing sponge that has a plastic tube you fill with detergent. You then hold the sponge by the tube and your hands will never touch the detergent.

It is sometimes easier to wash knickknacks made of china or porcelain than to dust them. Put a dish-towel in the bottom of the sink to keep them from chipping (good idea when you are washing glasses, as well).

Cleaning the bathroom is always a chore!

❏ Get a squeegee on a long handle so you can clean the shower stall or bathtub without bending or reaching.

❏ Flat cola or Tang will get stains off the bath-tub and toilet.

❏ Clean tiled walls and mirrors with glass cleaner and paper towels.

❏ Use vinegar or rubbing alcohol to make mir-rors sparkle.

2

GOOF-PROOF YOUR KITCHEN

HINTS ON MAKING COOKING EASIER, SAFER, AND MORE FUN

Kitchens are all about pleasure—they are places where things first smell good and then taste good—but they can also be frustrating and dangerous. In this chapter, we will try to find our way through the maze of kitchen activities and figure out how to do things safely, easily, and painlessly so that you can rediscover the joy of cooking without having to struggle and worry.

THE RIGHT TOOLS

The ideal kitchen has

❑ a food processor—to chop, slice, grate, and mix

❑ a mixer on a stand—to beat, mix, and knead

❑ an electric potato peeler—to peel vegetables and fruit and to spin salad

Everyone knows about food processors and mixers, but life will never be the same again if you get an electric potato peeler. It makes family dinners a breeze and drying salad greens effortless.

CAREFUL NOT TO CUT YOURSELF

The risk of cutting yourself is reduced if you don't try to cut a moving object. Keep it still by using

❑ a cutting board with two or three nails sticking up from the surface—this can be dangerous, but it's better than slicing your hands. Keep corks on the nails when you are not using the board to prevent puncturing yourself.

❑ a device with long metal teeth that goes through what you are cutting

A device to hold fruit or vegetables while you slice them.

If you have difficulty slicing and dicing, try

❑ a knife with a right-angle handle

❑ a mandoline (slicer used by professional chefs, available at fine kitchen stores)

❑ semiprepared food that can be found, diced or sliced, at your supermarket

A knife with a right-angled handle.

Or avoid using knives altogether.

❑ Boil onions for a minute and the skins will slip off.

❑ Get a little rubber sleeve to peel garlic.

❑ Use a garlic press to mince garlic.

❑ Use shears to dismember a chicken or chop herbs.

❑ Slice and core apples for pies and puddings with an apple peeler.

❑ Peel *everything* with an electric potato peeler.

❑ Chop onions and slice and shred vegetables in a food processor.

FIRES AND BURNS

Burning yourself or your food, or starting a fire, is the real danger in the kitchen. Get a fire extinguisher and learn how to use it. Then, be careful. Here's how:

❑ If you are a bit forgetful, get a timer on a cord to wear around your neck and set it when you put anything up to cook.

❑ Use electric appliances with automatic shut-off devices. You can get coffeepots, electric kettles, cookers, frying pans, rice cookers, and ovens that turn themselves off.

❑ Use pot holders, not dish towels, to handle hot pots.

When you're cooking something greasy:

❑ Sprinkle a little salt in the frying pan to keep fat from splattering.

❑ Put a slice of bread in the broiler pan to keep fat from catching fire.

❑ Cook bacon in the microwave between two sheets of paper towel.

❑ Remove fat with a bulb baster.

❑ Transfer the food to a clean pan to finish the cooking and pour off the fat when it cools.

❑ Use a two-handed skimmer to remove fat from soups and sauces.

Putting the Fire Out

- ❑ Use baking soda or salt—not water—on grease fires.
- ❑ Use a fire extinguisher or water on wood, paper, or fabric fires.
- ❑ Any small fire can be smothered with a pot lid or a blanket.
- ❑ *Don't* use water on an electrical fire.

Keep Out of Hot Water

If you have any trouble at all with your hands, you should *never* pick up a heavy pot of very hot or boiling liquid.

- ❑ If you are cooking food like pasta or vegetables in boiling water, put a fry basket in the pot first and put the food in the fry basket. When the food is cooked, remove the basket and let the water cool before you pour it out.
- ❑ Get an instant hot water attachment for your sink. (This may not work for you if you have small children or absentminded adults in

your house who may scald themselves on the hot-water tap.)

❑ Use an electric coffee urn to boil water, or boil small amounts in the microwave.

KEEP TAKEOUT FROM TAKING YOU OUT!

The food you eat is supposed to be good for you, or at least not bad for you. Many seniors, who live alone or in small households, often eat leftovers. That's fine, so long as you treat the leftovers carefully.

If you bring food home from restaurants in Styrofoam containers, to avoid bacterial contamination:

❑ Remove the food from the container and put it into one made of glass or plastic.

❑ Chill it quickly (the Styrofoam is designed to keep food warm, which is exactly what you don't want to do).

❑ Label it with the date.

❑ If you aren't going to eat it in two or three days, freeze it.

Get a supply of

☐ plastic containers with see-through lids (you're more likely to eat the food if you can see it!)

☐ wooden clothespins to close plastic bags— easier for stiff fingers than twist ties

Avoid food hazards:

☐ Raw eggs (found in mousse and meringue) may give you salmonella.

☐ Scrub any counter touched by raw chicken, which carries salmonella.

☐ Mayonnaise, unrefrigerated until it's warm, may give you food poisoning.

☐ Defrost meat in the refrigerator or in the microwave, not on the kitchen counter.

COMFORT
AND CONVENIENCE

Your kitchen should be a comfortable place for you to work, which means that it should be designed to avoid the things you have difficulty doing.

If you have trouble bending:

❏ Get a refrigerator with the freezer on the top.

❏ Hang pots and utensils on a Peg-Board.

❏ Get a cooktop and a separate, wall-hung oven.

If it would be more comfortable to cook sitting down:

❏ Think about an under-the-counter refrigerator and separate freezer.

❏ Create a small workspace by putting a cutting board across an open drawer.

❏ Lower the height of your countertops.

❏ Get a sturdy TV tray or a computer keyboard stand to work on.

❏ Rig up a sling that hooks onto eyebolts on your counter and sit in it.

If traditional faucets and knobs are hard for you to operate, replace them with handles that can be nudged instead of grasped.

❏ Replace knobs on cabinet doors with rings.

To make dishwashing more comfortable,
rig up a sling and sit in it.

❑ Loop a dish towel through the handle of the refrigerator.

If you have trouble reaching into the back corners of cabinets:

❑ Get a few lazy Susans.

❑ Install sliding shelves.

❑ Use blocks of wood to create steps for small containers so you can easily see food stored in back.

❑ Arrange your pantry so everything is visible.

Arthritis and stroke can play havoc with your hands, but there are many utensils and tools to compensate for lost strength.

- ❑ If you only have one usable hand, a rocker knife enables you to cut your meat by yourself.
- ❑ Plastic frames with handles for containers of milk or juice make them easier to pour.
- ❑ Get a refrigerator container with a spigot for water or juices, and when you have a guest or a helper, ask him or her to fill it.
- ❑ Examine devices designed to open jars and bottles until you find one you can use easily.
- ❑ Keep seasoned flour in an empty spice jar that opens easily for tidy flouring of cutlets.
- ❑ To butter corn neatly, put a pat of butter on a square of bread and rub.

A rocker knife.

MAKING IT EASIER FOR YOURSELF

❑ Buy prepared food or salad dressing and spruce it up by adding a little grated lemon zest or a crushed garlic clove (use a garlic press).

❑ Use premade piecrusts, or make crumbles instead of pies.

❑ Get a mixer on a stand and use it when you bake.

❑ Use your toaster oven to bake small quantities. You won't have to bend to reach the oven, and the pans, being smaller, will be lighter.

❑ Use melamine dishes and mixing bowls for everything except egg whites.

❑ Reduce the strain on your hands by using smaller pots, but don't use lightweight ones for anything except boiling water—food burns too easily in flimsy pots.

❑ If after cooking, serving, and eating a meal you're too tired to clean up, put the dishes in a dishpan full of soapy water and leave them until morning.

WHAT'S FOR DINNER?

The purpose of all your activity in the kitchen is to produce good things to eat, but getting the food into your kitchen can be a challenge, particularly if you don't drive or you live far from a good market. Here is one of the best tips I can give you: Think about buying groceries and household goods every two months. Even if you have to travel by taxi, you have to do it only six times a year. Here is my two-month list. It will take you a few cycles to edit yours so the amounts are right and it includes all the things you need.

Two Months' Marketing for a Small Family

Canned Goods
    Soup
    Fish (tuna, salmon, anchovies)
    Juice
    Tomatoes

Tomato paste

Meals (hash, stew, etc.)

Pasta/Rice/Beans

Pasta

Rice

Beans

Frozen Foods

Meals

Vegetables

Fruit

Dessert

Condiments

Mayonnaise

Mustard

Ketchup

Salt/Pepper

Spreads

Jam

Honey

Soft Drinks/Juice

Coffee/Tea/Cocoa

Baking

Flour

Sugar

Spices

Mixes

Cereal

Hot

Cold

Snack Food

Paper Goods

Toilet paper

Tissues

Paper towels

Wax paper/foil/wrap

Trash bags

Cleaning and Laundry Products

Housecleaning

Dishwashing

Polishes

Soap

Bleach

Staples (I buy 5 pounds each.)

Potatoes

Onions

Carrots

Butter

Buy as much meat and bread as you have room to freeze.

If cooking isn't your thing—or for those days when it is just too much—you can still eat well without eating out if you survey available providers of cooked food.

❑ Is there a caterer near you who will deliver meals, either every day or by special order?

❑ If you would like the convenience of frozen meals and the taste of really good home cooking, look into a service called Food from Home, which provides wholesome meals, complete with bread and dessert, all ready to be popped into the oven or the microwave. Their phone number is (800) 235-7070, and they ship nationwide.

❑ If you need meals on a fairly regular basis, look into Meals on Wheels, which is available through your local agency on aging and charges on a sliding scale. In addition to food, you get to see the volunteer who delivers it, which is nice too.

3

HOT ZONE OF HOUSE HAZARDS

WAYS TO MAKE YOUR BATHROOM MORE CONVENIENT AND SAFER

In many ways, your bathroom is the most essential room in your home. You can have all your meals sent in and do without a kitchen; you don't need to garden. But there is no way to get through the day without using the bathroom frequently. Unfortunately, the bathroom is also the most dangerous room in your home. However, there are many ways to make it safer, and if you have any physical limitations, you probably ought to make fixing the bathroom a priority.

SENIOR-PROOFING A SINK

❑ If the sink is mounted on the wall, it should have extra-strong brackets. They should be sturdy enough to bear your weight if you lean on the front edge of the sink. It is better to have a sink that is attached to a cabinet or vanity.

❑ If ordinary faucets are hard for you to grasp and turn, you can get adapters or handles that can be nudged rather than grasped.

MAKING YOUR THRONE FIT FOR A KING OR QUEEN

❑ If your toilet is a standard model, it is probably too low and positioned in the room so there is nothing to lean on to help you sit and stand. You can get special seats with backs and arms that both elevate the toilet and give you something to lean on to help you stand up. Some of them even have catapult seats! These seats range in price from $25 to $150.

❑ Safety frames, which will keep you from falling off the toilet seat, can bring the cost up to a few hundred dollars.

❑ Be sure the toilet paper is easy to reach without twisting or stretching.

❑ If refilling the roll has become bothersome, you can replace your current toilet paper holder with the kind that sits on a counter and allows you to drop the new roll over a center peg.

SOLVING THE SHOWER

❑ If you have an ordinary shower, there is almost certainly a ledge at the front of it. This may be a problem for you to get over and can easily cause you to trip.

❑ If you can deal with the ledge, all you need to do is install a sturdy grab bar.

❑ If you can't deal with the ledge, you can replace your existing shower with a prefabricated one that comes with no ledge, grab bars, a seat, and a handheld shower. This will cost you a few thousand dollars.

❑ If you replace your existing shower, try to get one large enough to accommodate a wheelchair should any member of your family ever need one.

❑ You may want to put a plastic chair inside the shower, or install a retractable seat, so you can sit while showering.

❑ A handheld shower (which can easily replace a fixed shower head), is a help and is almost essential if you shower sitting down.

BATHTUBS

If you can't replace your bathtub with a stall shower:

- ❑ Get a seat that straddles the edge of the tub— you sit down and wiggle across to the tub. Some of these can be folded out of the way if you share your bathroom with others.
- ❑ Get a fiberglass tub liner with a flat rim—you sit on the rim and hoist your legs into the tub. These cost about $200.

No matter how you arrange your bathing, you should have a device installed by your plumber to prevent the water from getting scalding hot, either

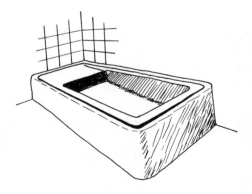

A fiberglass bathtub liner.

A seat that straddles the edge of the bathtub.

because you inadvertently move something or because the water system in your home has a hiccup. (This will, incidentally, protect everyone in your household from scalding.)

AVOIDING FALLS

It's easy to slip and fall in the bathroom. Install grab bars

- ❑ along the side and at the ends of the tub
- ❑ around the shower stall a little higher than waist height
- ❑ near the sink and the toilet

Be sure they are sturdy enough to bear your weight.

The safest floor covering for bathrooms is carpeting, even if it has to be replaced frequently. It keeps you from slipping and helps avoid shattered glass if you drop a glass bottle on the floor.

Be sure you have a skid-proof bathmat to keep you from slipping in the shower or bathtub.

Your bathroom should have

❑ a telephone

❑ a timer to hang around your neck to remind you the bath water is running

❑ open shelves for storing toiletries and medicines where you can see them

4

LOOKIN' SPIFFY

HOW TO CARE FOR, CHOOSE, AND GET INTO YOUR CLOTHES

How you dress tells a lot about how you feel about yourself. Looking attractive and neat and clean gives the world the message that you are someone valuable, and that's why you're well packaged. You don't wrap the garbage in gift paper! So it is particularly demoralizing when you find that you can't take care of your clothes the way you'd like and, worse yet, you can't put them on.

Although dressing is one of the activities of

daily living with which many people eventually need help, getting such help often involves a significant change in your lifestyle. If you want to delay making that change for as long as possible, you need to pay close attention to your clothes and, perhaps, make some changes in the way you dress.

CLOTHES MAKE THE MAN AND WOMAN: REASSESSING YOUR WARDROBE

Some things may be impossible for you to get into without help. Unless help is at hand, maybe you need to discard

- ❑ clothing that goes over your head—replace pullovers with cardigans
- ❑ clothing that buttons in the back, unless you can replace the buttons with a zipper or with Velcro
- ❑ shoes with laces

❑ jewelry that requires dexterous hands, like pierced earrings with separate backs and necklaces or bracelets with fussy catches

❑ neckties that have to be tied

REPLACING AGILITY WITH INGENUITY

Do you have limited mobility in your arms and shoulders that makes it difficult to get into jackets, cardigans, shirts, or dresses? Here are some tricks:

1. Clip onto the center of the collar at the back of the garment a wooden clothespin with a spring to which you have attached a piece of strong string several feet long.

2. Put your arms through the sleeves all the way, so that your hands come out at the end of the sleeve.

3. Place the string over your shoulder and let it hang down your chest.

4. Pull gently on the string, and the back of the garment will eventually settle on your shoulders, where it belongs.

If stiff fingers make buttoning difficult:

❑ Get a button hook to pull the button through the hole.

❑ Avoid having to button shirt cuffs by taking your shirts to a tailor (or a friend who is clever with a needle) who can attach the buttons to the shirt with elastic thread—there

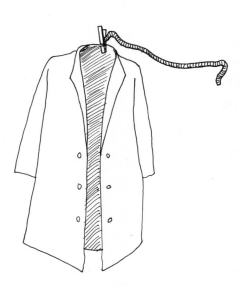

Getting into a garment if you have limited mobility in your arms and shoulders.

should be enough give so you can get your hands through the cuffs without unbuttoning them.

❏ If you like French cuffs, make cuff links of two buttons attached by elastic thread.

Zippers, especially on the back of dresses, can require you to be a contortionist!

❏ Buy a hook that fits into the hole in the zipper tab (if your zipper tab doesn't have a hole, replace it with one that does) and pull.

❑ If you have trouble reaching the hook, thread one end of a long piece of string into the hole and pull it through the hole until you have a double string hanging over your shoulder and down your chest. Pull the zipper up with the string and then pull on one strand to get the string out of the zipper. (It is easier to thread the string through the hole if you first stiffen the end with glue or nail polish.)

SHOES

Shoes and stockings perhaps require the most ingenuity of all.

❑ If you can manage it, don't wear shoes with laces. Choose slip-ons or shoes with flaps that fasten with Velcro instead. If laces are a must, get elastic ones.

❑ Can't reach your feet? Let your feet reach you, by placing them on a small stool, or get an extra-long shoehorn.

❑ If putting on socks or panty hose is a problem for you, there are devices that help. They are generally plastic frames, which hold the sock open, to which long ropes or rods are attached. You pull the sock up with the ropes, and the device slips out after you have gotten the sock past your heel.

Putting on your socks.

CONVENIENCE CLOTHING

Before you buy any clothing, think about whether it will be troublesome to put on.

Choose:

- ❏ pretied ties (clip-on ties)
- ❏ necklaces that are long enough to go over your head
- ❏ clip-on earrings

SPOT REMOVAL

Part of being well dressed is getting your clothes clean and pressed and keeping them that way.

- ❏ The sooner the better. Immediately after spilling something, dab it off with a little cold water or soda water. If you wait a few weeks, you'll have a project on your hands.
- ❏ Cold water probably won't hurt anything, but don't use more than you have to. If you use it on velvet, you may need to steam the spot (over a kettle) after it dries.
- ❏ Don't use salt on dark stains such as red wine. All you'll do is get the water out of the stain, leaving the dye behind. It will get paler, but what's left will be much harder to remove.

RETIRE YOUR IRON

Even clean clothes don't look good if they are rumpled. But if you have any problem with your hands, irons are dangerous to use.

❑ Irons are heavy and hot, and steam irons are full of hot water as well.

❑ The best way to avoid dropping an iron is never to pick one up!

❑ Instead of ironing the wrinkles out of your clothes, when you take a garment off:

1. Hang it up carefully.

2. Spray all the wrinkles with water (keep a spray bottle of water in your closet or in the bathroom).

3. Leave it undisturbed to dry.

❑ If the garment is very badly wrinkled, or is made of a fabric like linen that creases, it may help if you smooth the wrinkles between your fingers after you spray them.

❑ Renew the creases in trousers by smoothing them between your fingers while damp.

TIPS FOR TRAVEL

❑ Take a spray bottle with you (and a hair dryer if you think you may need to dry something quickly after you've sprayed it).

❑ If you fold clothes, pack tissue paper in the folds.

❑ Clothes left in plastic dry-cleaning bags don't crease as badly, whether they are folded or carried in a hanging bag.

❑ Roll garments instead of folding them.

GROOMING

E ven if you have physical problems, there are many ways to make grooming easier.

❑ Don't deal with screw caps. Buy brands that come in plunger or squeeze bottles or transfer any lotions or oils you use to plastic plunger bottles. (Save plunger bottles so you have them on hand when you need them.) The top never needs to be replaced on a squeeze bottle of toothpaste, and the tube never needs to be rolled up!

❑ Get a lighted magnifying mirror so you can see what you are doing when you put on makeup, put in contact lenses, and do anything else to your face.

❑ Get a nail brush that attaches to the sink with suction cups to clean your nails.

❑ A long-handled bath brush helps you scrub your back without twisting.

❑ Make the handles of your toothbrush and hairbrush fatter and more comfortable to hold. How to do it is discussed in Chapter 5.

❑ There are devices that help you hold razors, combs, or toothbrushes with weak hands by strapping them to your wrists.

A device to strap your razor to your wrist.

A hairbrush that is easier to hold.

Finally, buy services. It's okay to spend a little money taking care of yourself! Just because you have always done something for yourself doesn't mean you must continue to do so if it is difficult for you or if you are no longer able to do it well. Your life might be easier if you periodically went out and

❑ had your hair shampooed or set or colored

❑ treated yourself to a manicure and pedicure

❑ had your legs waxed instead of shaving them

❑ got made up by a professional makeup artist before a big party

❑ had an old-fashioned shave at a barber shop

AN OUNCE OF PREVENTION

If you don't get your clothes soiled, you don't have to get them clean. That may mean wearing an apron, or spreading your table napkin on your lap with care. It may even mean tucking it under your chin. If you have problems with incontinence, wear protective garments so your clothes don't get soiled and your bed linen doesn't have to be changed and laundered daily. Although you may feel awkward about some of these things, remember that nobody else cares or is even likely to notice. What people *do* notice is unsightly stains and unpleasant aromas.

5

MAKING YOUR GARDEN GROW

**HOW TO CREATE BEAUTY
AND STILL FEEL WELL
ENOUGH TO ENJOY IT**

Gardening, more than almost any activity I can think of, means different things to different people. Some people like nothing better than to spend every Saturday puttering in their flower beds. Others find pulling weeds twice a month an unbearable chore. But because of its infinite flexibility, no matter what is the matter with you or how little time you have to devote to the task, there is some form of gardening you can still do. It is important to focus on this, because all too often we hear people, growing old in their houses, remark that it's not keeping up the house that they find overwhelming, it's keeping up the grounds. If that's how you feel, it's time to take another look at the grounds.

For the sake of convenience, let's break this subject into three parts: keeping the grounds attractive, having a pretty garden to enjoy, and how to accomplish get-your-hands-dirty gardening even if you can't lift, bend or grasp.

THE GROUNDS

If you have always spent a great deal of time and energy on your grounds (mowing lawns, clipping hedges, pruning trees, planting and weeding) but recently have found these jobs to be more than you can handle, now may be the time to relandscape. Just because you can't do everything you used to do doesn't mean you can't do anything. Let not the best be the enemy of the good!

Lessen the Amount of Work Your Grounds Require

- ❑ Replace some or all of the lawn with another type of ground cover to cut down on mowing or raking.
- ❑ Instead of the hedges, mark your boundaries with fencing or trellises.
- ❑ Replace large shrubs and bushes with smaller ones.
- ❑ Keep your shrubs natural—they were never meant to have geometric or animal shapes!

What You Can Grow, or Establish, and Not Mow

- ❑ ornamental grasses
- ❑ a field of wildflowers
- ❑ a Japanese rock garden

Cover some of the area that used to be lawn with pebbles, bark, decorative stones, or brick. Make a curved path out of flagstones. If you are in a wheel-

MAKING YOUR GARDEN GROW

chair or use a walker, a concrete path may prove useful.

Five Easy Ground Covers

- ❏ sweet woodruff
- ❏ ivy
- ❏ pachysandra
- ❏ clover
- ❏ moss

Make What Lawn You Have Easy to Mow

- ❏ Make it round or oval in shape.
- ❏ Avoid right angles—frequent changes of direction are sure to throw your back out.
- ❏ Trees, flower beds, and birdbaths are hazards to navigation.
- ❏ Keep it flat—it's hard to mow uphill.

One of life's ironies is that when you construct a patio in order to avoid the upkeep of a lawn, you find that grass grows between the bricks of the patio like it never grew before. Here are a few ways to have a grass- (and weed-) free patio:

- ❑ Put black plastic under the brick when it is constructed.
- ❑ Kill the grass with boiling water, a strong solution of bleach, or a garden chemical like Roundup.
- ❑ Get a long-handled hoe to dig out the grass and weeds.
- ❑ Plant a fragrant ground cover, like wild thyme, to grow between the bricks. It will give off a lovely aroma when you walk on it.

A Work-Free Front Yard

- ❑ Replace the grass with gravel, seashells, wood chips, or pavement.
- ❑ Grow a few dramatic or colorful plants in large pots.

Cut Flowers Instead of Hedges

- ❏ Replace the hedge with a fence.
- ❏ Grow climbing roses or flowering vines on the fence.

Six Flowering Vines

- ❏ clematis
- ❏ wisteria
- ❏ jasmine
- ❏ silverlace
- ❏ honeysuckle
- ❏ trumpet vine

GARDENS

Once you get the grounds under control, you must decide what you want to do in the way of gardening. What are your real limits? What can you do and what do you want to do? It is important for you to be honest, at least with yourself, because whatever your limits are, you can garden within them, but if your garden is going to work it really has to be tailor-made to you. If, for instance, you have trouble walking, seeing, or bending or lifting, you can still garden, but the garden will be set up differently to take account of what you can't do or can do only with difficulty.

Water Gardens

For flowers with *no work at all*:

1. Choose a container
   - ❑ a Victorian bathtub
   - ❑ a child's wading pool
   - ❑ a whiskey barrel with a liner
   - ❑ a bucket
2. Fill it with water and put in some
   - ❑ water lilies
   - ❑ papyrus
   - ❑ small floating ferns

3. Make it more elaborate with
   - ❑ a fountain
   - ❑ fish
   - ❑ a spotlight

Perennial Gardens

If your life has changed and you expect to make trips away from home during the growing season, or if you just don't want to do a lot of work anymore, you can have a genuinely work-free perennial garden that provides you with flowers from spring to fall.

- ❑ Plant hardy perennials that grow easily in your area.
- ❑ Install an automatic watering system.

Outwit weeds by
- ❑ dense planting
- ❑ lots of mulch
- ❑ plants with large foliage that will shade the ground beneath them

To weed without bending over, sit in a beach chair.

Raised Beds

If you like to do real, dirt-under-your-fingernails work in your garden, but bending or kneeling for any length of time is a problem for you, think about having a raised bed constructed so that you can garden sitting down. (An incidental benefit of raised beds: If you grow fragrant flowers, the aroma is closer to your nose as you walk by!)

Build your raised bed on a structure of

- ❑ soil
- ❑ concrete blocks
- ❑ brick
- ❑ wood

Conceal the sides with

- ❑ trailing vines
- ❑ trellises
- ❑ stockade fencing

Top the structure with a wooden box eight to twelve inches high and braced at the corners. (Be sure the wood hasn't been treated with a toxic substance, especially if you're growing vegetables.)

The dimensions of the box should be

❑ less than two feet deep (an easy reach for your arms)

❑ ten to twelve feet long

Design it with a

❑ flat border to sit on

❑ surrounding path of brick, concrete, or wood if you're in a wheelchair

Locate it

❑ near the house

❑ with an eastern or southern exposure, for the best sun

❑ so that the plants don't shade each other as the sun crosses the sky

Finally, equip it with an automatic watering system with a computerized timer.

Container Gardens

If permanently installed raised beds are not practical for you, think about gardening in containers. You can grow virtually anything in containers that you can grow in a regular garden, and they have many advantages.

Make sure your containers are easily moved by putting them on a

❏ wheelbarrow

❏ wagon

❏ dolly

Then, your containers can

❏ follow the sun

❏ be protected from wind and weather

❏ come indoors when the air gets chilly

Vary your landscape by

❏ displaying flowering plants when they're in flower

❏ removing from view plants that are in a dormant stage

Plant your container plants in
- ❏ whiskey barrels
- ❏ cachepots
- ❏ decorative old tin cans
- ❏ baskets

Fill the container with
- ❏ special container soil mixes
- ❏ a layer of Styrofoam pellets for drainage if the container is large

Grow fruits and vegetables as well as flowering and foliage plants.
- ❏ With full sun, you can have peppers, squash, eggplant, and tomatoes.
- ❏ A few hours of sun are ideal for lettuce, cucumbers, radishes, beans.
- ❏ Herbs need less water and nutrients, and much less space, than vegetables.
- ❏ Strawberries in hanging baskets and fruit trees cut down trips to the grocery store!

If you have no outdoor space, or if being out in the sun is a health problem for you, you can have an indoor garden

❑ on a sunny windowsill

❑ under a Grow-lite

Make plants the decorative focus of your room.

❑ Group them in an old Victorian crib or a non-working fireplace.

❑ Add a fountain and let the water trickle down rocks.

Container gardens are easy to keep healthy.

❑ Inspect new plants for evidence of insects or disease.

❑ Keep containers off the ground and inaccessible to pests.

❑ Water and feed them frequently—easy with an automatic system.

❑ Put a layer of charcoal or pebbles in the bottom of the pot for drainage.

TOOLS OF THE TRADE

Whatever kind of garden you have, if you are going to work in it, you need tools. Fortunately, there is equipment available for people with every kind of physical problem, and there are also ways to adapt equipment you already have.

If you can't bend, or if a few hours in the garden leave you with an aching back, there are many tools with long handles:

- ❑ weed pullers
- ❑ bulb planters
- ❑ shears
- ❑ trowels

If you want to work in a sitting position, get

- ❑ a stool on wheels
- ❑ a low beach chair
- ❑ long-handled tools made for children

Be sure that your garden is

- ❑ surrounded by a flat surface on which the wheels don't get stuck
- ❑ on level ground

If you prefer getting closer to your plants by kneeling:

- ❑ Protect your knees with padding.
- ❑ Be sure you can get up—get a stool with handles to help.

Never lift or carry heavy things. Get

- ❑ a wheelbarrow
- ❑ a wheeled cart

and use it to carry

- ❑ bags of soil or fertilizer
- ❑ tools and equipment

Get a gadget that permits you to sweep or rake leaves or debris right into a trash bag.

If you have arthritis in your hands and grasping is difficult for you:

- ❑ Buy tools with fat rubber handles.
- ❑ Adapt the tools you already have by wrapping their handles with soft padding such as
  - ❑ weather strip
  - ❑ air-conditioner filter material
  - ❑ toe bandages

- ❑ foam innersoles
- ❑ bicycle handlebar grips
- ❑ cane tips
- ❑ clay
❑ Use duct tape to attach the padding to the handle.

Look for padding ideas in
❑ the plumbing section of a home improvement store
❑ the foot care section of your pharmacy
❑ a surgical supply store

Weather strip.

Air-conditioner filter material.

Foam innersoles.

Bicycle handle grip.

Clay.

Materials to help adapt your tools.

❏ the clay section of a store that sells crafts supplies

One benefit of adapting your own tools is that as your grasp gets better or worse you can make the padding fatter or thinner.

If you have a problem with your wrists:

❏ Buy tools with trigger grips.

❏ Use the strength of your arm by attaching tools to your forearm with

   ❏ an elastic bandage

   ❏ a harness

   ❏ a glove

Attach your tool to your forearm with elastic bandage.

With a glove.

WATER

It is essential that you find ways to get water to your garden without having to haul it. Remember that a pint weighs a pound, and you need a great many pints to water even a small garden. Instead, think about

- ❏ drip irrigation kits for container gardens
- ❏ sprinklers and soaker hoses for in-ground gardens and lawns
- ❏ automated timers for watering when you're away from home

For convenience:
- ❏ Keep hoses near plantings.
- ❏ Get lightweight watering cans.
- ❏ Get a "quick release" fitting to connect your hose to a sink faucet and run the hose through an open door or window.

MAKE YOUR GARDEN A PLACE YOU LOVE TO BE IN

Make birds feel welcome in your garden by planting

- ❏ trees
- ❏ holly
- ❏ bittersweet
- ❏ grapes
- ❏ trumpet vines

Butterflies love clumps of flowers, especially red ones:

- ❏ asters
- ❏ zinnias
- ❏ sunflowers
- ❏ coneflowers

If you can't see well, you might enjoy

- ❏ wind chimes that sing in the breeze
- ❏ a burbling fountain
- ❏ flowers chosen for their fragrance

- ❏ vivid and contrasting colors
- ❏ bigger, taller flowers
- ❏ paths of different materials to help you orient yourself
- ❏ a garden situated near the house so you don't have to strain to see it

If you're in a wheelchair, design a garden with
- ❏ dimensions that allow you to get around it easily
- ❏ room to turn around
- ❏ paths that are easy to ride on

GET YOUR
MOTOR RUNNING

**TIPS ON DRIVING
AND ON NOT DRIVING**

Most Americans believe that a combustion engine is a vital organ and don't think it is possible to survive without one in the driveway. Some older drivers take life-threatening risks every time they get into the car because they view the loss of their ability to drive as almost the worst catastrophe that can befall them. In this chapter we are going to look at ways to prolong your ability to drive, signals that it's time to stop, and solutions to the problem of how to cope without a car.

IT'S NEVER TOO LATE TO LEARN

Take a course!

- ❑ 55 ALIVE/Mature Driving is given by AARP.
- ❑ Defensive Driving is given by the National Safety Council.
- ❑ An added bonus—in many states, graduates of these courses get a reduction on their insurance premiums.

REASSESS YOUR SKILLS

Maybe you can still drive safely, but not

- ❑ at night
- ❑ in bad weather
- ❑ during rush hour

❑ on high-speed, limited-access highways

❑ on winding country roads

Safe driving may require more attention now, so when you're behind the wheel, don't

❑ eat, drink, or smoke

❑ talk on the telephone

❑ carry on an animated conversation with a passenger

❑ listen to an absorbing radio program or tape

❑ travel with unruly children or animals who require discipline or attention

❑ go to unfamiliar places where you are likely to get lost and become distracted looking for the right road

REASSESS YOUR EQUIPMENT

Car manufacturers are aware of some of the problems that face older drivers and for decades have worked on finding ways to solve them because it enables them to sell more cars. Find a car dealer who is willing to work with you on making your car safe and convenient for you.

As of this writing, General Motors will reimburse you up to $1,000 for the installation of special equipment in a new GM car that makes it easier or safer for you to drive. The only requirement is that the equipment not be offered as a standard option on the car you are buying. Ford and Chrysler have similar programs.

Here are some of the things that are available:

Getting In and Out

- ❏ Try a swivel seat.
- ❏ Install handholds to help pull yourself up or steady yourself.
- ❏ If you're tall, the seat of a van may be at a more convenient height for you than a car.
- ❏ Getting out of a van may be easier if you can step down onto a small stool.
- ❏ Not all car seats are at the same height. Shop around for one that works for you.

Car Seats

❑ Cushions, lumbar supports, head rests, and seat covers are available to make the seat more comfortable.

❑ There are adapters that will help you if you feel as if the seat belt is strangling you.

❑ Get a cushion to boost you up if the seat is so low that you can't easily see out of the windows.

Good Gadgets

❑ If the air bag deploys while the front seat is as far forward as it will go, you may be seriously injured. Pedal extenders allow you to keep the seat at a safe distance and still reach the pedals. Be sure you don't get so far back that your arms can't steer easily.

❑ If turning to see if there is somebody in your blind spot is difficult for you, get a supersize rearview mirror to eliminate the blind spot.

❑ Increase the effectiveness of your sun visor by installing a gadget that has a pull-down screen for glare and an attachment that makes the panel nine inches wider.

❑ Grasping the steering wheel may be difficult if you have reduced hand strength. Install a knob or a special covering on your steering wheel to make it easier.

See Chapter 8 for safe-driving aids for the hearing-impaired.

BAD-WEATHER DRIVING

Even if you try to avoid driving in bad weather, it will happen, particularly if you live in a region where the weather changes rapidly. To be prepared, be sure you have

❑ good windshield wipers, and replace the blades frequently

❑ clean glass covering your headlights and tail-lights; dirty glass cuts down on available light

❑ a heated windshield, but get an ice-scraper too

❑ snow tires, chains, or front-wheel drive to enable you to drive safely on ice and snow

❑ a bag of kitty litter in case you get stuck on ice

❑ a blanket and a flashlight in the car, for emergencies

Safety Tip: A car phone enables you to call for help when you need it. There are inexpensive plans for people who use them only in emergencies.

SELF-HELP

If you have trouble finding dials and switches in the dark, put a bit of glow-in-the-dark tape on the ones you need to see:

❑ the dial that turns on the lights

❑ the windshield wiper wand

❑ the directional signals

❑ the 55 mark on the speedometer

WHERE DOES THE CAR END?

If you have trouble staying in a lane, would it help to have a hood ornament? Hardly any cars come with them, but you can buy them at auto supply stores. It might make it *much* easier to drive.

WINDOWS STEAMED UP?

In damp weather, moisture sometimes condenses on the inside of your windows and you can't see. Turn on the air conditioner and they'll clear in a jiffy. (You can turn on the heat too, if it's chilly.)

PERPLEXING PANELS

Instrument panels on some cars look as if they belong on supersonic jets. Choose a car where the dials are simple and are clustered so you can see them easily even if your peripheral vision is poor.

KNOWING WHEN TO STOP

It is important to stay calm and try to be sensible when you consider whether it is time to stop driving. Even though you have taken the courses and restricted your driving and equipped your car, the day will come when that isn't enough. Instead of focusing on what you will do if you can't drive (we'll come to that soon), pay attention to what may happen if you continue to drive. Wherever you're headed, it's not worth dying for. Nor is it worth killing for. How would you feel if you killed a child because you didn't see him or her? It happens, and you don't want it to happen to you.

If you, or a friend or relative, are concerned about your ability to drive, don't let the question become an emotional hot potato—get a professional opinion. Hire a certified driving instructor to give you a road test. Driving tests for seniors are also administered by the Centers for Disease Control, the National Institute on Aging, AARP, and the National Highway Traffic Safety Administration. If you fail the test, you really shouldn't be driving.

The National Safety Council suggests that it's time to stop when you

- ❑ have frequent fender benders
- ❑ can't see at night
- ❑ have poor peripheral vision
- ❑ can't distinguish colors
- ❑ get lost on familiar routes
- ❑ can't concentrate well
- ❑ drive too slowly for road conditions
- ❑ have trouble staying in a lane
- ❑ turn from the wrong lane
- ❑ stop at green lights and intersections
- ❑ confuse the gas pedal and the brake pedal
- ❑ are taking a lot of medication

HOW TO COPE WITHOUT A CAR

You might be more willing to stop driving if you had an idea of how to live without a car. Most Americans can't get anywhere without wheels, but they don't have to be *your* wheels.

1. Make a list of all the places you needed a car to get to in the last month.
2. Survey the resources available to you.
   - ❑ Do you have a friend who goes to your church or is on your committee who could pick you up and take you home with no great inconvenience?
   - ❑ Does the local senior center or agency on aging provide transportation to shopping or doctor's appointments?
   - ❑ If you have a car, can you find a someone in your community you could hire to drive you around for an hour or two a few times a week? How about a high school or college student?
   - ❑ Is the grocery or pharmacy willing to deliver telephone orders? That also solves the problem of getting the groceries in the house.
   - ❑ Can you arrange with the local taxi company for a few hours every week at their slow time of day?

3. Think about ways to make your life more efficient. Chapter 3 discusses how to buy staple groceries every two months and other ways to get food without driving.

PUTTING THE PRICE IN PERSPECTIVE

Most people who don't live in big cities never think of taking taxis because they cost money. But so do cars, and you might be surprised at how many taxis you can take before it begins to cost more than maintaining a car. To calculate:

1. Figure out how much your car cost you last year—add up payments, insurance, maintenance and repairs, gas, and any other costs (like tickets!).
2. Divide the total by 52—that's the amount you can spend each week on taxis or delivery charges before it begins to cost more than driving yourself.

II
Special Challenges

7

WHEN THE WORLD BEGINS TO GROW DIM

TIPS ON COPING WITH FADING VISION

All of us, as we get older, see less well than we used to. Virtually nobody past fifty can read without a little help from reading glasses, and most people need increasing amounts of light and magnification. For some of us, the problem is much worse, but if misery loves company, we're all in this one together.

POOR VISION RESPONDS TO LIGHT AND MAGNIFICATION

- ❑ Many people can read the newspaper without glasses in bright sun. Nobody can read the menu in a dimly lit restaurant.
- ❑ Even if you don't think of yourself as visually impaired, it is always sensible to have with you a small flashlight and a credit-card-size magnifier.

WAYS TO BRIGHTEN YOUR LIFE

- ❑ The less well you see, the more important it is that your home be well lit.
- ❑ Use contrasting colors, especially at danger points like stairs or thresholds.
- ❑ If the furniture and the carpet are all the same color, or even shades of the same color, you may have trouble differentiating them.

❏ Don't choose monochrome meals. You may not be able to find white food on a white plate. Use a colored plate and you are back in business.

❏ Identify the color of clothes (especially black, navy, and brown, which can look alike in poor light) with tags. If you won't be able to see the tags, put tiny safety pins in an inconspicuous place—one for black, two for navy, three for brown.

If your peripheral vision is deteriorating:

❏ Don't rearrange the furniture.

❏ Get into the habit of being tidy.

❏ When doing a task, keep all the tools or utensils you need in one place.

LIGHTS FOR SPECIAL TASKS

❏ Light should be focused on the object to be illuminated—the book, the papers, the keyhole.

103

- If you cook, install lights under the wall cabinets so you can see the counter or stove.
- Your desk should be equipped with a good desk lamp and perhaps an illuminated magnifier.
- A necklace flashlight will light up the book or knitting in your lap.
- To avoid glare, choose adjustable lighting, like dimmer switches and three-way bulbs.
- Cover shiny surfaces or use nonglare wax.
- Install window shades to block the sun.
- Out-of-doors, get sunglasses that block ultraviolet light and wear a brimmed hat.

THE WORLD OF MAGNIFIERS

- Magnifiers come in all shapes, sizes, and strengths.
- Some are handheld, some come on stands, some have lightbulbs built into them.
- For work that involves the use of both your hands, get a magnifier designed to hang

*A magnifier attached
to a visor.*

*A magnifier designed
to hang around your neck.*

around your neck or attached to a visor that
you wear on your head.

❑ There are special-purpose magnifiers for putting on makeup and doing crafts.

❑ You can get a magnifier to enlarge the image
on your TV.

WHEN LARGE PRINT
ISN'T LARGE ENOUGH

❑ If you need extreme magnification, you can
get an electronic magnification system. You
scan the printed material with a handheld

camera, and it appears on the monitor screen magnified up to forty times its original size. An attachment allows you to magnify your handwriting as you write. The system costs about $3,500, and the handwriting attachment is $750.

❑ There are several electronic systems, some in color, that use your television screen as a monitor. One of these is portable. These systems are somewhat less expensive but rarely under $1,000.

MAKE YOUR EARS SEE FOR YOU

If it is easier to get information through your ears instead of your eyes:

❑ There are many watches, clocks, and alarm clocks that announce the time as well as show it to you.

❑ You can get talking calculators, key rings, and compasses.

❑ For your health-care needs, you might like a talking blood glucose monitor, blood pressure monitor, scale, or clinical thermometer.

❑ If identifying currency is a problem, you can get a gadget that tells you the denomination of any U.S. currency from $1 to $100. Another adds bills for you.

❑ Finally, there is the world of talking books, including cassettes of thousands of recent bestsellers, available in bookstores and libraries.

HELP FOR THE VISUALLY IMPAIRED

❑ large-print newspapers and books

❑ everything with buttons—remotes, calculators, telephones, thermostats, thermometers, toaster ovens—can be found with extra-large buttons

❑ supersize playing cards and bingo boards

❑ clocks, rulers, and kitchen timers with large numerals

- ❏ tape measures with ridges you can feel
- ❏ writing guides, designed for checks, envelopes, and sheets of paper
- ❏ needle threaders, some of which thread sewing machine needles
- ❏ a guard device to put on your iron so you won't burn yourself even if you can't see it very well

IS BRAILLE FOR YOU?

If your eyes are very bad, you might want to use your fingertips instead and seriously think about learning Braille. The hardest thing about learning Braille is admitting to yourself that you need to. If your vision isn't going to improve, Braille opens a whole new world to you and makes many things easier. It is yet another example of the maxim that you can do anything you ever could do—you just may have to do it differently. Braille gives you back your ability to write and read what you've written, so you can still make lists and write reminder notes to yourself. You will be able to label things and read the labels, deal with your medications, play many board games—in short, do most of what you ever could do.

FREEDOM IS A THREE-LETTER WORD: DOG

Legally blind people, if they meet certain criteria, can get guide dogs who not only see for them but love them as well.

- ❑ You must be able to get around with a white cane.
- ❑ You must be oriented in your home and anywhere else you spend time.
- ❑ You must be in reasonably good physical condition—able to walk a few miles a day.

At Guiding Eyes for the Blind, in Yorktown Heights, New York, after the dog has been trained there is a twenty-six-day, live-in, human/canine training program where the pair learns to work together and negotiate all kinds of terrains, weathers, and situations—including escalators and malls.

❑ There is no charge for any of this (although the cost to Guiding Eyes, from puppyhoood to graduation, is $25,000 per dog).

❑ There is no age limit—a woman in her late eighties graduated last year.

❑ Having another physical problem besides blindness is not a bar, as long as the problem doesn't interfere with your ability to walk.

8

DID YOU SAY SOMETHING?

HELP FOR THE HARD-OF-HEARING

O f all the ills that befall us as we get older, the one about which we are most likely to be unreasonable is loss of hearing. People who have worn glasses for most of their lives and thought nothing of it turn cartwheels to avoid wearing hearing aids. This is really not very smart. Loss of hearing

❑ makes you miss much of what is going on around you

❏ makes people scream at you (and even if they are not angry to start with, screaming makes them angry)

❏ exposes you to risks every time you walk out of your house

If your hearing loss can be corrected with hearing aids, *get them!* If hearing aids are a help but not a solution, there are many mechanical aids that will help.

Wear a receiver that vibrates or flashes a light when signals are sent to it from

❏ telephones

❏ doorbells

❏ pagers

❏ doors or windows opening

❏ smoke detectors

❏ fire alarms

❏ sound monitors

Each of these devices can be obtained separately as well.

For ease in using the telephone:

❏ Get a device that amplifies and clarifies sound (some newer phones have this built in).

❑ Use a special typewriter to have conversations on the phone (you can even get a portable one to use with pay phones!).

Amplifying and clarifying systems are available for meetings and social gatherings, a particular problem for people with hearing loss.

Get a listening system for your radio or TV.

You can get an alarm clock that wakes you by vibrating the bed or flashing lights.

DRIVING

❑ Get a device that alerts you to the presence of emergency vehicles. It flashes lights that become more intense as the sound gets closer.

❑ Can't hear the directional signal when you have inadvertently left it on? You can get a device that amplifies the sound or one that flashes a light.

❑ If you have a car phone, you can get a vibrator to tell you it's ringing and an amplifier that makes it easier for you to hear.

- ❏ You can get an amplifier to help hear the radio and conversations that are taking place in the car.
- ❏ An oversize mirror will allow you to see what's going on in the backseat and to lip-read conversations (but not while you're driving, please!).

CONVERSATION—HOW TO DO IT DIFFERENTLY

If you would rather rely on yourself than on a lot of gadgets, learn to lip-read.

- ❏ It will make conversation easier, especially in places where assistive devices are apt to be ineffective, like social gatherings.
- ❏ It will put you, and not an arsenal of technology, in control of your life.
- ❏ It won't break or need a new battery.

THE ULTIMATE ALLY

Hearing loss can expose you to real danger every time you walk out into the street. Many warning signs are auditory, from a shouted, "Look out!" to alarms, sirens, and horns. It is really dangerous for somebody who is profoundly deaf to go out into the street alone, and it is not altogether safe to stay home alone either. The solution? The Hearing Ear dog.

Hearing Ear dogs tell you when

- ❏ the doorbell rings
- ❏ the baby cries
- ❏ the microwave pings
- ❏ an alarm goes off
- ❏ somebody calls your name

They run back and forth between you and the source of the sound until you tell them to stop. Like all intelligent working dogs, they also consider unfamiliar sounds and let you know about them.

Because this is a high-energy job, Hearing Ear dogs are usually small terriers, dogs that are both smart and energetic. Wearing special orange collars and leads, they can go anywhere a Seeing Eye dog can go, which is pretty nearly everywhere. In addition to making a dangerous world safe (a tall order for anybody, especially if it weighs less than fifty pounds), they are among the best friends and companions in the world.

How to get one? Call NEADS at (508) 422-9064 or the Delta Society (206) 226-7357. They both have locations nationwide.

9

GETTING AROUND GETTING AROUND

WHAT YOU NEED TO KNOW

ABOUT WHEELS

I f you need a wheelchair or a walker to get around and you feel burdened by it, it might help to put the whole thing in perspective and remember that during many impressionable years of your childhood, the president of the United States was in a wheelchair. He certainly managed to get around! While it is undeniably a nuisance, it really isn't a catastrophe. And it certainly beats being housebound.

The Americans with Disabilities Act has made the outside world a much easier place for wheelchairs and walkers to navigate.

❑ It requires that places of public accommodation (which is a very broad range of commercial establishments) be accessible to people with disabilities.

❑ It mandates barrier removal, which involves installing ramps, making curb cuts, moving shelves and telephones, installing flashing alarm lights, widening doors, and changing door hardware.

❑ If a facility near you is not in compliance, you can register a complaint by contacting the municipality where the facility is located.

It is up to you to make your private world more convenient as well. Equip the device you use to move around with trays, baskets, and other conveniences. Carrying liquids while using a walker can be impossible without a tray or cupholder. Your hands are not available for holding things, so be sure the wheelchair or walker is.

Unless your need for a wheelchair or walker is temporary or very intermittent, it is worth a considerable amount of effort and expense to make your home accessible.

❑ Seated in a wheelchair, you can easily reach about four feet ahead of you and to your sides and almost a foot up or down.

❑ Light switches in your home should be installed at a height that you can reach.

❑ Or consider some of the lighting options, like motion-sensor lights and toggle switches, discussed in Chapter 1.

❑ You might like a lamp that goes on when you touch any part of the lamp, or a lamp you can click on with a transmitter.

❑ If you go in and out alone, your lock may have to be lowered so you can reach it.

❑ Be sure that there are clear pathways that allow you to get around.

❑ Have a comfortable chair surrounded by enough space that you can easily get into from your wheelchair—a wing chair is a good choice.

ROOM TO MANEUVER

In order to maneuver easily in a wheelchair, you have to consider four things:

1. the width of the door
2. the space in front of the door
3. the weight of the door
4. the hardware

EXITS AND ENTRANCES

It may not be necessary for you to get through every door in your home (the guest room, for instance), but you must be able to get through

❑ the doors to rooms you actually use

❑ at least two doors to the outside, in case of fire

DOORS

To accommodate a wheelchair, a doorway must be at least thirty-two inches wide.

❏ If you can do without the door, remove it and, if the opening is still not wide enough, cut away the bottom section of the door-frame.

❏ If you can't do without the door, replace the hardware with hinges that swing clear of the doorframe—this will give you an extra one and a half to two inches.

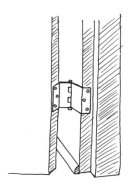

Hinges that swing clear of the door frame.

A door requires two feet of empty space to open.

❏ If your door opens out onto a landing, you may not be able to get your wheelchair far enough away to make room for the door to open. Can the door be rehung so it opens into the room?

❑ Replacing your regular doors with sliders, pocket doors, accordion doors, or swinging doors may be ways to solve your problem.

Doors to the outside must be sturdy.

❑ If you have trouble opening heavy doors, install an automatic door opener like the ones often found on garage doors.

❑ Ways to make a door safe include strong hinges, a good lock, a handle—preferably of the lever variety—and a peephole at wheelchair eye level.

STORAGE

C losets and shelves that you use daily must be designed so you can reach them. You can find these systems in catalogs and at big home improvement stores.

Think modular!

❑ Install long, narrow brackets on the wall.

❑ Hook into them hanging rods and shelves that come on special brackets (in the kitchen you can use them for countertops, cooktops, and sinks, too).

❑ If you share your closet with others, you can have some of the hanging space at one level and some at another.

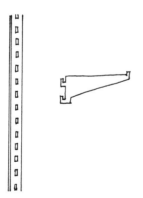

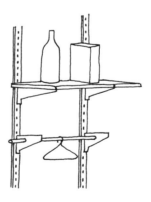

Think modular! Long, narrow bracket and shelf support.

Shelf and hanging rod that can be moved up or down to suit your needs.

THE KITCHEN

I f you cook, make the kitchen wheelchair friendly.

❑ The cooktop and the sink should be mounted on the wall with no cabinets under them so you can get close to them in your wheelchair.

❑ A freestanding table, high enough for you to get close to, provides a work surface.

❑ If your sink is uncomfortably deep, a rack on the bottom will raise the level so you can reach things.

Cooking equipment doesn't mean a stove.

❑ Look for a cooktop with staggered burners so you can reach the back ones safely.

❑ A flat, radiant-heat cooktop may be best.

❑ Be sure you can reach the controls without reaching over a hot pot—it may be easier if they are on the front, not the top.

❑ A wall oven at a convenient height may be the best choice, but be sure you can deal with the way the door opens. Conventional oven doors drop down. You may prefer a convection oven or a microwave with a door that opens to the side.

❑ Get an inexpensive wooden gadget that looks like a giant crochet hook to pull out oven shelves. It will keep you from having to reach into the oven.

You can reach the controls and the rear burners without reaching over a hot pot.

Storage is always a problem in kitchens, and eliminating the base cabinets makes your problem even harder.

❑ Be ruthless in deciding what you are going to give houseroom to!

❑ Try using Peg-Boards on the wall or racks that hang from the ceiling.

❏ If you have room for it, get a portable cart.

❏ Keep your long reachers handy.

THE BATHROOM

For people in wheelchairs, the bathroom is the most difficult room in the house. (It's not exactly easy for seniors in general!) Chapter 3 discusses ways to adapt your bathroom, but in addition:

❏ Mount the sink on the wall or, if you can't, remove the door from the base cabinet or vanity.

❏ Replace the faucets with levers so you can reach them more easily.

❏ Have the hot water temperature adjusted so it is never scalding.

The easiest way to transfer from the wheelchair to the toilet is to put the chair next to the toilet, but there is rarely room in most bathrooms to do that. At a minimum you should:

❏ Install grab bars to help you with the transfer.

❑ Raise the level of the toilet seat.

❑ Install strategically placed grab bars to help you get up.

Bathing is a challenge.

❑ The easiest solution is a stall shower designed to accommodate a wheelchair.

❑ You can put a chair in the shower you have and transfer into it, but you still may have trouble with the ledge at the bottom of the shower—eliminating it requires a plumber.

❑ If you love to take baths, or if soaking in the tub is part of your regime to stay flexible, you need a seat that allows you to transfer from your wheelchair to the tub—this is not an easy exercise! Be sure to have grab bars.

SERVICE DOGS

A general assistant, always eager and willing and never complaining, is available to help you. It is called a service dog. Service dogs, usually

Labrador retrievers, are trained to assist people in wheelchairs by

- ❏ opening doors
- ❏ turning on lights
- ❏ picking up things you have dropped
- ❏ fetching things
- ❏ carrying things

Interested? Call NEADS at (508) 422-9046 to discuss how you can get one.

10

WHAT WAS IT YOU SAID?

**WAYS TO IDENTIFY—
AND COPE WITH—
MEMORY LOSS**

Few things are as frightening as memory loss. We are so afraid of it that we sometimes invent it, sort of making our worst nightmares come true. Memory loss is a problem for many of us, but we should first put the problem in perspective, then consider ways to head it off and finally ways to cope if it really happens.

NOBODY'S PERFECT— WHY SHOULD YOU BE?

Not long ago, an eightysomething friend looked at the wrong page in his engagement book and panicked that he had dinner guests coming. When he realized his error, he decided that senility had set in. My twentysomething daughter, on hearing the story, said, "You know, everyone does that sometimes. The only difference is that when I do it, I think I've been careless. When he does it, he thinks he's getting senile." None of us is perfect, and the occasional mistake or spell of absentmindedness only proves you're human.

THERE'S A LOT IN YOUR MEMORY

❏ You've been storing information in your memory since the day you were born, and that was a long time ago.

❏ The longer it's been there, the more secure it is. What we tend to lose is short-term memory, like the name of the person you just met. Long-term memory, and even recent memory, like what happened last week, are less likely to be affected.

❑ When you try to recall something, in order to find it you have to sort through more data than you did when you were twenty or thirty or forty. It only stands to reason that it will take longer, but you will find it eventually.

❑ The best way to deal with slowing down is to stay calm.

WHAT'S NORMAL AND WHAT'S NOT?

It's okay if

❑ you forget names of people you just met
❑ you can't think of a word on the spot (but it comes to you later)
❑ it takes a little longer than it used to to make choices or decisions

But pay attention if you

❑ forget how to get to or from places you visited often

❑ can't manage to follow instructions, like directions or recipes, that you used to be able to follow

❑ don't remember what you did today

❑ keep repeating the same stories to someone

❑ can't handle money

❑ experience a change in personality, like becoming grumpy, anxious, confused, or less well groomed

WHAT DOES IT ALL MEAN?

Memory loss can indicate

❑ normal aging

❑ dementia

❑ your drugs and medications need to be adjusted

❑ you are depressed

Dementia tends to get steadily worse over time. Other causes of memory loss change much less quickly. You need to see your doctor to rule out medications and depression as a cause of memory loss.

USE IT OR LOSE IT

❏ Brains benefit from exercise. Studies have shown that symptoms of real disease, like Alzheimer's, are often masked in people who use their brains a lot.

❏ Find some mental calisthenics you can do every day—try the crossword puzzle.

❏ If you can, read and take courses to exercise the gray matter.

PAY ATTENTION

❏ A great deal of what we "forget" we never really learned properly in the first place.

❏ When you are introduced to someone, repeat his or her name. You won't remember it if

you hear it while you are worrying about
whether the cat will get out the open door or
if you are scanning the room to see if your
sister-in-law is there.

❏ Be sure that the problem isn't that you didn't
hear or see something because you need new
glasses or a hearing aid.

MAKE LIFE EASIER
FOR YOURSELF

There's a great deal you don't have to remember
if you use your head.

❏ Answer invitations the minute they arrive
and write them in your book so you don't
have to remember whether you responded
and when the party is.

❏ Get a bulletin board and pin up tickets, invitations, and announcements by month—
then you'll be able to find them.

❏ Write things on the grocery list as soon as
you use them up, and take the list with you
when you go marketing so you don't have to

remember whether there's any bread in the house.

❑ Return phone calls as soon as you get the message. If you do it now, you don't have to remember to do it later.

❑ Arrange automatic payment of monthly bills, so you don't have to remember them.

Let Post-its or yellow stickies save your sanity! Write yourself reminder notes and put them where they will really remind you.

❑ The minute you hear on the morning weather forecast that it may rain, write "umbrella" on a sticky and put it on the door where you'll see it as you leave.

❑ Keep a list of important dates in your life—birthdays, anniversaries, and the like—and put a yellow sticky on the telephone that says "Milly's birthday" to remind you to call.

❑ Or, on the first of every month, send cards to everyone who is having a birthday that month. It's better to send a card early than late or not at all.

❑ Keep a pad of stickies and a pencil in the car. When you begin to run low on gas, write "buy gas" on a yellow sticky and put it on the steering wheel.

PUT THINGS IN THE WAY

Errands and chores are not very memorable, so we tend not to remember them. It might help to hang a string or plastic bag on the doorknob.

❑ Shoes need to go to the shoemaker? Put them in the bag.

❑ Library books to return? Put them in the bag.

❑ Clothes need to go to the cleaner? Put them in the bag (or if they won't fit, on the floor under the bag).

ROUTINES

❑ Every morning, put your medications in a box designed to hold one day's worth of pills. Put the box on a kitchen counter or the table

where you eat lunch and dinner to remind
yourself to take the pills on schedule.

❑ Every morning, consult your engagement
book and write yourself notes to put on the
telephone, the front door, and the bathroom
mirror to remind yourself of things you are to
do that day.

❑ On the first of every month, write in your engagement book the birthdays and anniversaries that happen that month, so you won't
forget them.

LIMIT LOSSES

❑ If you tend to mislay your keys, your purse
or wallet, or your engagement book, get several special key chains that make a noise
when you clap your hands and attach one to
each of these items.

❑ Put things away where they belong. I know
it's a little late to reform, but the benefits of
neatness were never more comforting than
they are now.

III
Live a Little

11

MAKING SURE OUT OF SIGHT ISN'T OUT OF MIND

HINTS ON STAYING IN TOUCH AND STAYING IN CONTROL

DISTANT GRANDCHILDREN

Ever since the days when adventurous young people went west in covered wagons, American families have often been separated by long distances. This can be a source of pain and sorrow, especially when a member of the faraway group is a grandchild. But if your grandchild does move to Guam, all is not lost. Even if the grandchild is a baby, there are ways of keeping in touch between visits and of participating in his or her life as he or she grows up.

How you keep in touch with a distant grandchild depends, first of all, on how old the child is. If the child is a baby, too young to speak, read, or write, your response has to be different than if the child were on E-mail.

First of all, there is the telephone.

❑ Call regularly and speak to the child. (I know infants can't speak, but you would talk to an infant if you were physically present. Talk the same way over the phone.)

❑ Over time, the child will come to recognize your voice and, eventually, will learn to speak.

❑ If you can afford it, video telephone equipment is a wonderful thing to have, and the price keeps going down.

❑ A videophone allows you to see each other as you speak. You will be able to watch your grandchild grow and participate in exciting things like learning to walk, the first haircut, Halloween costumes, and Christmas morning.

In addition to speaking, you can exchange photographs and videos.

❑ Get into the habit of taking videos of yourself doing ordinary things—walking the dog, baking cookies for the grandchild, working in the garden.

❑ Have conversations with your grandchild on the tape—"Here's Rover chasing a ball" or "Look at Puss stalking that bird."

❑ If you are handy and can make gifts for your grandchild, video yourself making the gift and send the tape along as part of the present.

❑ Invite the child to do the same thing. It is comforting for you each to know what the other one's home looks like and to be familiar with friends, pets, and hairstyles.

When the child gets a little older, it is time to read stories.

❏ Whenever you buy a book for your grandchild, read it into a tape recorder. Then send the book and the tape. Reading stories to your grandchild can become a family tradition.

❏ You can send—and receive—other messages on tape. (I know a family that did this even though a memorable tape, made during dinner, seemed to have nothing on it but complaints that one person got more dessert than another!)

When the child becomes a toddler, it's time for interactive projects.

❏ Get a coloring book and two boxes of crayons. Color the sky and send the book and one box of crayons to your grandchild. Ask him or her to color the trees and send the book back to you. When you finish a picture, send a frame so your grandchild can display your joint work. (You can also work jointly on pictures to illustrate stories you've read together.)

❑ Games, like ticktacktoe, checkers and, eventually, chess, can be played together by mail.

❑ Buy a book of riddles and send them, one at a time, in letters.

❑ If your letters contain something that's fun to do together, they are even more exciting for your grandchild.

By the time your grandchild gets to grade school age, it's probably time for you to get a computer and a modem and learn about the mysteries of E-mail. (It's really not very mysterious!)

❑ For people separated by long distances, it is a wonderful and very inexpensive way of staying in touch. You can exchange mail of any length for the cost of a local phone call.

❑ If there isn't a time zone problem, you can make dates to be on-line together. This allows you to type messages and instantly get your grandchild's response. More sophisticated computers can even transmit your voice—just like a telephone only without the long-distance rates.

WHAT WAS IT LIKE WHEN YOU WERE A CHILD?

One of the many things you have to give to your grandchildren is a link to their past.

❑ You knew ancestors of theirs whom they will never meet.

❑ You remember family homesteads and favorite vacation spots that are gone now.

Write it down! Written family histories are precious records of an age that is past. Writing a family history need not be a daunting task. Think of it as if you were telling a grandchild what it was like when you were little.

❑ Who were the people and animals who populated your life as a child?

❑ What were they like?

❑ Where did you live and what did your home look like?

❑ What were your favorite foods, games, books?

❑ Tell about your favorite teachers and the subjects you liked and didn't like.

❑ Was your school big or small?

❑ Describe your town and how you got around in it. Did you walk? Bike? Ride the trolley?

❑ When did your family get a car?

❑ What did you do on vacations?

Describe growing up.

❑ Your first job, your romances, your marriage.

❑ The really interesting things aren't grand achievements but everyday events. Were you ever naughty? What did you do? Did you ever experience any of the same things as your grandchild?

❑ How old were you during World War II and how did it affect your life?

Talk about the birth and growing up of your children, your grandchildren's parent and aunts and uncles.

❑ How were they like your grandchildren and how did they differ?

❑ Finally, tell them how excited you were when they were born and how happy you are that they are your grandchildren.

If you write a little every day, your family history will be done in no time. It might be the impetus you need to purchase and learn to use a computer, but if you prefer to write it by hand or on a typewriter, that's fine too. If you have a child or grandchild who is good at computers, perhaps he or she can type and duplicate it. Otherwise, take it to a copy shop and have copies of it made for all of your children and grandchildren.

WHO'S TO KNOW?

If something happened to you, who would know? And how would they find out? These are important questions, and if you live alone, it is essential that they be answered.

❑ Which friend or relative do you want to be informed in the event of an illness or accident?

❑ Try to choose someone who lives nearby as the person to be informed.

❑ Or choose somebody who is easy to find—a housebound friend or a child whose business life requires frequent checking of telephone messages, wherever in the world he or she is.

❑ That person should be given a list of those you wish advised of your condition when you can't do it yourself.

The harder question is how is the stranger who finds you after an automobile accident or after an attack of some kind going to know whom to call?

❑ If you are an orderly person who never goes out into the street without your purse or wallet, a card saying, "In case of emergency, call . . ." will do.

❑ If, like most people, when you go out to walk the dog or pick up a loaf of bread you carry no identification, you might think about wearing an ID bracelet with your name and the "In case of emergency . . ." information on it.

❑ If you wear an emergency call pendant (and if you live alone, you really should), you will have given the company the name of your child or your doctor or your neighbor.

Emergency call pendants take a great load of anxiety off you and your family. You can get one through a dealer listed under "Medical Alarms, Systems & Monitoring" in the Yellow Pages. If you need any kind of help, all you have to do is push the button.

Another way of making sure that if you need help you will get it is to make an arrangement with a friend to telephone each other once or twice a day or, if you can see each other's windows, to watch for lights going on and off at appropriate times. If you have a friend who drives by your home to and from work, you can ask him or her to glance at the lights to make sure the outside light has been turned off in the morning and on in the evening.

GETTING YOUR WAY

Sooner or later, it is likely that you will have a bout of serious illness. Before that happens, make sure somebody in your family knows what you want done, in the event you can't make medical decisions, and is empowered to see that it gets done.

❑ Appoint somebody your health care agent by a document called a health care proxy.

❑ Have a living will so that when your agent is asked how he or she knows what you want, the agent can produce the living will with your instructions.

❑ You can appoint only one person your health care agent, but you can name alternates if the person you choose is unable or unwilling to act.

This is not a pleasant thing to think about, but it is infinitely worse to have a course of treatment that is contrary to your wishes and not be able to do anything about it. If you don't want to go to your lawyer for this, your state bar association can furnish you with forms for living wills and health care proxies.

AFTER YOU'RE GONE

Eventually, we all die. What happens to your property after you die depends on two things—your will and the tax collector.

❑ It is important that you have a will; otherwise the law divides up your estate, and it may do so in a way you wouldn't like. Your will should be drawn by a competent lawyer who also supervises its execution.

❑ This is not a time to do it yourself. If you make a mistake, it won't be possible to correct it.

In addition to drawing up your will, your lawyer should help you with estate planning.

❑ You can minimize estate taxes and deal with the matter of where the money is going to come from to pay the estate taxes.

❑ Particularly if your assets are tied up in things you would rather not have your heirs sell, like a family business or a family home, you need to provide for the payment of taxes out of some other assets.

❏ Life insurance is often an appropriate way to arrange for sufficient liquid funds to pay taxes.

❏ Sometimes it is appropriate to start giving away certain assets before you die.

Because this is a complicated matter and there are financial and tax, as well as personal, consequences to whatever you decide to do, you should seek competent and independent advice. Don't go for advice to anyone who has a financial interest in your choosing one solution rather than another. To get advice that's good for you, you want to ask someone who gets paid the same amount of money whatever you decide.

As a final gift to those you leave behind, you should arrange your affairs so that they are easy to understand.

❏ A folder with the names and phone numbers of your attorney, accountant, insurance agent, and financial adviser, your bank and investment account numbers, and instructions concerning your wishes for your funeral will be an immense help to your family.

❑ If you have prearranged your funeral, as discussed in the next section, details of that should also be in the folder.

It will probably make you feel better if you don't leave an untidy mess, and it will certainly make life easier for your loved ones.

FUNERALS

Funerals are the third most expensive thing many of us ever buy, after a house and a car. Typically, we arrange for a funeral when we are grief stricken and not in a mood to bargain. That makes us easy prey to the suggestion that the opulence of the funeral is somehow a measure of how much we love the deceased, and we are made to feel guilty if we even *think* about money; after all, this is the last thing we are ever going to get to do for dear old Dad. Inasmuch as death is an absolute certainty, it seems prudent to arrange for your own funeral in advance, when everyone is calm and thinking clearly, and to encourage your family members to do the same.

Of course, it is very difficult to do this, because although we all know we are going to die, it's not something we like to think about. We can never find the "right" time to discuss the matter with our nearest and dearest, because they are sure to be upset at the very mention of the subject. That being the case, maybe the thing to do is take the initiative and do it alone—either because you really want to be in control of your last rites or because you want to relieve your immediate family of a difficult and upsetting job.

You should start by having a talk with your minister (or priest or rabbi), if you have one, and with a local funeral director. Ask whether your religious group has any cooperative venture, like burial societies, that may help arrange your funeral. After you have a good idea of what the alternatives are and what they cost, you can prearrange the whole funeral. If you want assurance as to price, you can even prepay, but be sure that you are comfortable that the funeral home will still be in business when it is time to deliver on this agreement. If you don't prepay, the price may change between the time you sign the contract for services and the time you need the funeral. If you want to be buried in a cemetery, the purchase of the plot is a separate transaction.

Although your funeral is really for the benefit of those you leave behind (you, after all, will no longer care about such things), it is a help to them to know what you would have wanted. If you have done a careful job, you will have made your wishes clear, down to the hymns, the flowers, and the charity designated for donations, if you'd prefer that to flowers.

12

CASH IN ON YOUR YEARS

MAKING YOUR MONEY WORK FOR YOU

Next to health, people worry more about money than any other subject. We worry about running out of money and about losing it as a result of trickery or fraud. Many of us feel anxious about dealing with what, on some days, seems like a world full of people—some honest, some not—who are interested only in taking money from us. In this chapter we will look at ways to protect your money and ways to make it go farther.

SCAMS

A week rarely goes by without a frightening headline in the newspaper about some new scam aimed at, among others, senior citizens. Having worked hard all your life to accumulate money, what can you do to be sure it won't be stolen from you?

There are only a few kinds of scams, although there are an infinite number of ways of promoting them. Once you understand what they involve, you'll recognize the most common scams, which ensures that you will not be easy prey.

Here are six rules that will keep you safe from scams.

- ❏ *Never* send money to somebody you don't know.
- ❏ *Never* give your credit card number, bank account number, or social security number to someone who calls you on the phone and asks for it.
- ❏ *Never* withdraw money from a bank and give it to somebody you don't know.
- ❏ *Never* call a 900 number to find out about a prize you have won.

TELEMARKETING FRAUD

Telemarketing fraud is big business. The Illinois attorney general's office reports that it costs Americans about $40 billion a year. The FBI estimates that 10 percent of telemarketing companies are fraudulent and that nearly 80 percent of the crooked companies target seniors. We are attractive targets because

- ❏ We are accustomed to buying things over the phone and find it convenient, especially if getting around is a problem.
- ❏ We have been brought up to be nice and polite. We feel rude when we hang up the phone on somebody.
- ❏ Many of us have a lot of leisure time to fill, and reading mail and talking on the phone seem like good ways to fill it.
- ❏ Many of us are lonely, and crooked salespeople call and visit, which may be more than anyone else does.
- ❏ Many of us are worried about money, and probably everybody would like to have more of it.

❏ Even though we may worry about money, we often have spare cash to spend.

Common Telemarketing Frauds

❏ You have won a "free" prize, but you have to pay money to get it. Sometimes what you are supposed to pay is the tax on the prize. Sometimes you have to attend a "seminar" (this is another opportunity to sell you something you neither need nor want). Other times you are asked for a credit card number. Sometimes you are asked to make a very expensive phone call to a 900 number to verify the prize.

❏ You have won a "free" or "bargain" vacation. If the vacation happens at all, which it seldom does, it will not be as described and will likely cost you more than a vacation you planned.

❏ You are offered something you need, like vitamins, at what is said to be a bargain price. It often comes with a prize. If you really do need the product, you can almost certainly get it for less money elsewhere. As to the prize, if you ever see it, it won't be much.

❑ You are offered an investment opportunity that is guaranteed to make you rich. Frequently, the opportunity will disappear tomorrow, so you are asked to send money overnight. There is no such thing as an investment that is guaranteed, and high-yield investments are always high risk as well. If it sounds too good to be true, it almost certainly is.

❑ Some charity, whose name sounds sort of familiar and whose story is designed to make grown men weep, needs your money. Like the investment scams, these people need it today, and they would rather have it in cash.

❑ Finally, if you've fallen for any of the above, you will probably hear from somebody who offers to get back what you've lost. The reason they know so much about what was stolen from you is either that they are the people who stole it or they are in league with the crooks. Don't throw good money after bad.

You can protect yourself from telemarketing fraud by taking your time, asking for information in writing, and never giving credit card, social security, or bank information over the phone. Simply saying, "That's very interesting. Could you please send me written material so I can discuss this with my spouse [or child or lawyer or financial adviser]," is guaranteed to make them go away.

HOME REPAIR FRAUD

More complaints filed with the attorneys general and the Better Business Bureaus concern home repair than any other subject. Even when the contractor is honest, there are endless opportunities for misunderstandings and dissatisfaction. So how do you tell the difference between an honest contractor and a crook? Here are some clues.

❑ A salesperson or a contractor comes to your door to tell you that something in your house needs to be fixed. Sometimes he offers to do the job cheaply because he has "materials left over from another job." He wants you to sign a contract on the spot, or give him money on the spot. (He may even offer to drive you to the bank to get the money.)

❑ A contractor offers to "inspect" your house for you. You can be sure he will find something that needs to be fixed, and it may well be that he is also taking the opportunity to look around in preparation for a burglary he's planning.

❑ Someone who claims to be an inspector or some other kind of official comes to inspect your property and then tells you there is some dangerous condition that must be corrected at once and offers to do the work for you or get it done.

If you think you need home repairs, you should initiate the action.

1. Get three estimates from contractors you have selected.
2. Get references and *check them*.

3. When you have selected one, put in writing
   - ❑ what is to be done
   - ❑ how much it will cost
   - ❑ how long it will take
   - ❑ whether there will be penalties for late completion
   - ❑ when payment is to be made (Some payment should be withheld until the job has been completed to your satisfaction.)

It is a good idea to have a lawyer review the contract. Although it may seem like a simple matter, if there is ever a dispute about the project that makes you choose to withhold some payment the contractor thinks is due, you may find that a mechanic's lien has been placed on your property.

If someone comes to the door, thank him or her for his or her interest, ask for a card, and say you'll be in touch. (Check the card to see if it has an address as well as a phone number.)

SWEEPSTAKES AND PRIZES

It is much more likely that you will be struck by lightning than that you will win $10 million. Yes, people do win sweepstakes, and it might be you, but if it is, it *will not cost you any money*. That should make you think, when somebody tries to get money from you.

- ❑ All sweepstakes are run in conjunction with selling something. (Do you really think there is some gigantic tooth fairy in the sky who gives away millions of dollars every year just out of kindness and generosity?)
- ❑ Sweepstakes cannot require you to buy to enter, and the honest ones tell you that.
- ❑ All that small print on the form that boldly announces "You have won $10 million if . . ." may be a way of tricking you into making an unintended purchase—most likely a subscription, health product, or phone service.
- ❑ You won't realize what you've done until you start to get bills for whatever you ordered.

❏ Read the form until you find the procedure for entering if you don't order. Then follow it, unless you really want what is being sold.

DON'T SEND MONEY — OR SPEND IT

You may be informed by a sweepstakes company that you have won a prize, and that you must

❏ call a 900 number (which costs money)

❏ pay shipping and handling (sometimes they ask for a credit card number for the shipping and handling)

The only valuable prize sweepstakes companies distribute is money, and that won't cost you anything. If you have to pay for it, you don't want it.

GRANNY FRAUD

This is a really creative scam practiced most frequently on older women, hence the name. The way it works is this:

- ❏ You get a phone call from someone claiming to be either a police officer or a bank examiner.
- ❏ He or she tells you that the authorities need your help to trap a dishonest bank employee at a bank where you indeed have an account.
- ❏ You are asked to go to the bank and withdraw a sum of money and bring it to a rendezvous, usually in a parking lot. Sometimes you are asked to do this more than once.
- ❏ *Don't*. This is not how dishonest bank employees are caught, and you will never see your money again.

REVERSE MORTGAGE CONSULTANTS

A reverse mortgage is not a scam. But recently, "experts" in reverse mortgages have been charging hefty commissions for "helping" seniors find reverse mortgage lenders. All they do is give you the list of lenders you can obtain, free of charge, by sending an SASE to the National Center for Home Equity Conversion, 7373 147th Street, West Apple Valley, MN 55124. Before you agree to pay someone for services, find out what the services are.

GETTING WHAT'S COMING TO YOU

These days, *entitlement* is getting to be a dirty word, and we are constantly being told that we are going to pauperize the next generation by collecting the financial support that's been promised to us. That's nonsense. Entitlements, like Social Security and Medicare, are benefits we spent decades paying for. They are prepaid insurance, not a handout.

It's a good idea, just before you reach the age of sixty-two, to call or visit your Social Security office to see what your entitlements are.

- ❏ You can start to collect Social Security at sixty-two, but Medicare doesn't start until you are sixty-five.
- ❏ You may choose to delay receiving Social Security payments up to age seventy (the longer you wait, the bigger the payments will be).
- ❏ If you are still working, ask about the rate at which your income will reduce your Social Security payments.
- ❏ If you are divorced, you may be entitled to collect under your ex-spouse's Social Security.
  - ❏ The marriage must have lasted at least ten years.
  - ❏ You must have refrained from remarrying until age sixty if your ex has died, or until sixty-two if your ex is still alive.
  - ❏ You can't collect both yours and your ex's, but you can collect the larger one.

It is also a good idea to visit your area agency on aging to see what other benefits may be available to you. Some, like a discount card for public transport, are available to everyone. Most other benefits, however, have a rather stringent means test that looks at your income and/or your assets to determine eligibility. Although they vary from place to place, there are typically up to fifteen things that you can get help with—from food stamps to assistance heating your home.

DISCOUNTS

Once you've figured out how to get all the money that's coming to you, the next step is to see how far you can make it go. The world is full of discounts for seniors, and the definition of "senior" varies from fifty to sixty-five. Frequently, simply asking how old you have to be to be a senior gets you the discount!

Virtually all transportation—planes, trains, cruise ships—offers senior discounts, some of them substantial. There are sometimes restrictions, so check to make sure that the trip you're planning doesn't run afoul of them.

Airfare on a Budget

Airlines sell senior coupons; a book of four costs just under $600, and each coupon is good for one trip within the continental United States. (Hawaii is counted as two trips.) Whether this is a bargain depends on a few things.

❑ Is the cheapest available fare to your destination less than the approximately $150 the discount coupon will cost you? (Don't forget, every stopover is treated like a separate trip, while regular airline tickets generally allow some stopovers.)

❑ Will you to be able to use four coupons in the space of a year? (You can, as a practical matter, extend that to two years by buying tickets on the last day of the first year, each of which will be good for twelve months.)

❑ If your travel involves regular trips to one destination, either to go between homes with the seasons or to visit a child or grandchildren, coupons may save you a lot of money. If you never seem to travel on the same airline twice, you may wind up buying coupons for which you have no use.

Saving Money on Entertainment

- ❑ Retail stores offer senior discounts, often on their slow days. If you can manage to do your shopping on those days, you will save money.
- ❑ Restaurants frequently offer discounts, generally during their slow hours, so you may have to eat early to get them.
- ❑ Movie theaters and museums almost always offer discounts, as do some concerts and theaters.
- ❑ Sports events sometimes have discount prices for seniors.
- ❑ At many ski resorts, lift tickets get less expensive as you get older, and after age seventy or so, are free.

In a world that changes as rapidly as ours, an exhaustive list of discounts would be obsolete before the ink was dry, so it is a good plan always to ask. Most people do not volunteer that they give senior discounts for fear of offending you. But you get paid to ask, so ask. You are whatever age you are and there is nothing you can do to change that. If somebody is offering you a reward for being your age, take it!

BARTER

Even better than getting things for less is getting things for no money at all. Barter is a wonderful system, and once you get into it, it has limitless possibilities.

Make an accurate and complete list of the services you need.

- ❏ somebody to phone morning and night to make sure you're all right
- ❏ someone to run errands for you in bad weather
- ❏ someone to walk your dog
- ❏ someone to weed the garden

Your list will be uniquely yours.

Once you have made your list, think about what you can do for a friend or neighbor.

- ❏ Does he or she travel? Perhaps you can feed the cat or water the plants when he or she is away.

❑ Is your neighbor a working mother? Perhaps in exchange for picking up a few things for you when she does her marketing, you can take a child to the movies once a month and give her an afternoon off. (This should be a firm offer. "I'd like to take Susie to the movies and out for a soda on Saturday. We'll leave at 1 and be back by 5," not, "Let me know if there is ever anything I can do for you.")

❑ Do you know how to do something somebody wants to learn in exchange for services, like how to speak a foreign language, use a computer, make pie crust, knit?

❑ Do you know how to do something other people may need done—rewire lamps, iron, sew, write a fine italic hand?

The only requirement is that you each get something that is of value to you, not that they take equal amounts of time or energy. If you put your mind to it, you may be astonished at the number of things you can do that will serve as barter for the things you need.

Appendix: Resources

If any of the equipment discussed in this book might help make your life easier, here is a list of places to find it.

Three Indispensables: Catalogs No Senior Should Be Without

Sammons Preston Enrichments   (800) 323-5547

An extensive catalog put out by a company that employs many physiotherapists, this is a gold mine of equipment designed to tackle all sorts of physical problems for those who need extra help to do things they might otherwise not be able to do.

adaptAbility   (800) 288-9941

This catalog has unusually innovative equipment to help you maintain an active lifestyle.

Silvo Home   (800) 331-1261

Concentrating on equipment for the home and the kitchen, this catalog offers an impressive assortment of mechanical helpers not found anywhere else.

Chapter 1: A Kinder, Gentler Place

Home Improvements   (800) 642-2112

Their claim that they provide "Quick and Clever Problem Solvers" is certainly true, particularly for electrical and lighting needs.

The Safety Zone   (800) 999-3030

As its name implies, this catalog is strong on equipment that makes you and your surroundings safer.

Preferred Living   (800) 543-8633

An unusually good collection of things that will make life around the house and yard easier.

Chapter 2: Goof-Proof Your Kitchen

The "Three Indispensables" are particularly helpful here; see also

The Good Idea	(800) 538-6690

My comment on this is "Excellent catalog." It is full of things I would love to have in my kitchen!

Home Trends	(716) 254-6520

Put out by the Fuller Brush Company, this is particularly strong on cleaning aids.

Chef's Catalog	(800) 338-3232

This catalog is full of equipment that makes cooking easier.

Kitchen & Home	(800) 414-5544

Full of innovative equipment that isn't found elsewhere, this catalog has many useful helpers.

Vermont Country Store   (802) 362-2400

The Bible of Yankee ingenuity, the products in this catalog are fun to read about and a real pleasure to use.

Chapter 3: Hot Zone of House Hazards

Dr. Leonard's   (800) 785-0880

This is a discount health care catalog with many inexpensive aids.

Chapter 4: Lookin' Spiffy

Mountainville House Calls   (800) 460-7282

This is a source for many useful gadgets.

SelfCare   (800) 345-3371

This catalog has a wonderful assortment of personal care aids.

Alsto's Handy Helpers   (800) 447-0048

Alsto's offers many practical products.

Chapter 5: Making Your Garden Grow

Preferred Living   (800) 543-8633

See Chapter 1 above.

Handsome Rewards   (909) 943-2023

This is a collection of unique and often useful gadgets.

Home Improvements   (800) 642-2112

See Chapter 1 above.

Vermont Country Store   (802) 362-2400

See Chapter 2 above.

Chapter 6: Get Your Motor Running

Home Improvements   (800) 642-2112

See Chapter 1 above.

The Safety Zone   (800) 999-3030

See Chapter 1 above.

Dr. Leonard's   (800) 785-0880

See Chapter 3 above.

Handsome Rewards   (909) 943-2023

See Chapter 5 above.

HARC Mercantile Ltd.   (800) 445-9968

(for the hearing impaired)

This is a remarkable catalog, full of equipment for the hearing impaired.

Chapter 7: When the World Begins to Grow Dim

The Lighthouse Catalog   (800) 829-0500

Published by the Lighthouse for the Blind, this catalog has a large assortment of equipment for the visually impaired.

Home Improvements   (800) 642-2112

See Chapter 1 above.

Handsome Rewards   (909) 943-2023

See Chapter 5 above.

Chapter 8: Did You Say Something?

HARC Mercantile   (800) 445-9968

See Chapter 6 above.

HearMore Products   (800) 881-4327

This is a very useful collection of equipment for the hearing impaired.

Chapter 9: Getting Around
Getting Around

The "Three Indispensables" are particularly help-ful here.

In writing this book, I found help and advice in the following books:

AARP. *Connections for Independent Living.*

AARP. *The Gadget Book.* Glenview, IL: Scott, Fores-man, 1985.

Better Homes and Gardens Gardening Tips. Des Moines, IA: Better Homes and Gardens Books, 1996.

Cary, Jane. *How to Create Interiors for the Disabled*. New York: Pantheon Books, 1978.

Hessayon, D. G. *The Easy-Care Gardening Expert*. Expert Books, published by Transworld Publishers, Ltd., London, 1996.

Jacobi, K. *Patios and Window Boxes*. Aura Books, published by Transedition, Ltd., Oxford, England, 1996.

Yeomans, Kathleen. *The Able Gardener*. Pownal, VT: Garden Way Publishing, 1992.

Index